THE POSITIVITY PAPERS

— Volume One —

By Jonas Cain

All rights reserved. No part of this book may be used or reproduced in any manner whatsoever without the written permission of the publisher unless you have a very good reason for doing so without such permission.

ISBN-9781792076527

First Edition © January 2019
This Edition © January 2020

Hashtag Positivity, LLC | Boston, MA

HashtagPositivity.com

HASHTAG POSITIVITY

Hashtag Positivity is a social entrepreneurship that supports emerging leaders and their influencers to develop resilience through a positive growth mindset, clarity of purpose, and high value relationships. Services include:

- Engaging keynote presentations and empowering workshops for conferences, annual and monthly meetings, school assemblies, campus events, and professional development in-service trainings.
- Online courses for independent study.
- Individual, team, and leadership assessments.
- Resources for ongoing inspiration and reinforcement.
- Positivity branded apparel to let positivity shine in everyday life.

If you or the people you lead are ready to experience the next level of enjoyment and excellence at school, work, home, and beyond, then get started today by taking the Positive Self-Assessment online. Best of all, it's free to give it a try!

HashtagPositivity.com

POSITIVITY

REVIEWS OF BOOKS BY THE AUTHOR

BEST BOOK!
"This is an amazing book with enlightening views on positive thinking. Love this book and would recommend it to anyone. Amazing!"

Kate / Amazon.com Reviewer

GREAT LOVE & TRUE EMOTION!
"From the first page, I was hooked. The author expressed such great love and true emotion. A tender and tragic story. Thank you for sharing your heart!"

Cari S. / Amazon.com Reviewer

TRULY INSPIRATIONAL!
"Incredibly empowered by this book. His spirit and love of life is truly inspirational. Highly recommend this book to anyone.!"

Heather Neal / Amazon.com Reviewer

REDISCOVERY OF HOW TO LIVE!
"This book contains all the required principles for living a happy life. It draws from a variety of excellent sources to instruct the reader in achieving their goals. I highly recommend you read and ponder it as a fine wine being tasted and enjoyed for the first time."

Vulcanicus / Amazon.com Reviewer

THE RIGHT INFORMATION!

"We all have tough times and everyone handles it differently. Jonas chose to use his experience to help others. This book came to me at an opportune moment. I just finished Making Things Happen, by Cathy Sticker, and this book picked up where I was left. Nicely done, Jonas. Keep up the good work!"

Julie / Amazon.com Reviewer

A LIFE-CHANGING BOOK!

*"*It Just Happened the Other Day *is an 'I can't put it down book and let me read it again!!!' It has life, love, joy, sadness, beginnings and endings— truly a book for young and old. It is a book that has to touch one's heart and open one's life to what love is truly about! It is an easy read but has great depth. A great gift for anyone! The best gift to yourself. It is life changing!!"*

Leah / Amazon.com Reviewer

HE DOES EVERYTHING WITH PASSION!

"The story he shared was inspirational…to show readers that even when you face the darkest times there is always a reason to forge ahead. I could connect with his words and it was well worth every page. Jonas is an incredible writer, magician and overall just a great person. Everything he does he does with passion and you will not be disappointed if you decide to read his book or attend one of his shows."

Liane Muise

For You

CONTENTS

INTRODUCTION
WHAT DOES IT TAKE TO BE GRAND?
1

ISSUE 1
WATCH YOUR FOCUS
9

ISSUE 2
FIND THE GOOD IN ANY SITUATION
13

ISSUE 3
TURN YOUR IDEAS INTO REALITY
16

ISSUE 4
HOW TO OVERCOME ADVERSITY
21

ISSUE 5
IMPROVE YOUR ABILITY TO CONNECT
27

ISSUE 6
WHAT'S YOUR LEGACY?
34

ISSUE 7
STAY ENCOURAGED
39

ISSUE 8
INCREASE YOUR CONFIDENCE
47

ISSUE 9
IMPROVE ENGAGEMENT
54

ISSUE 10
A HIGHER LEVEL OF HAPPINESS
60

ISSUE 11
PUT YOUR PLANS TO THE TEST
68

ISSUE 12
WHY POSITIVITY MATTERS
75

BONUS MATERIAL
THE 5 C'S OF EXCELLENCE
85

FINAL THOUGHTS
109

Photograph by H. Scott Photography

Contemplating Life
— May 6, 2018 —

*Our true selves are revealed
in what we love and in what we hate.*

*I love you because you reflect
that which I love in myself.*

*And if there is anything I hate,
it is because I see reflected in it
some aspect of myself that I hate.*

— **JONAS CAIN**

INTRODUCTION
What Does It Take To Be Grand?

Geologists estimate that it took anywhere from 6 million to 70 million years for the Grand Canyon to become the wonder that it is today.[1] Can these numbers even truly be fathomed? It literally took *millions* of years for this Wonder of the World to be endowed with the title "Grand." Such a large number is truly inspiring, offering us a valid excuse to go easy on ourselves when we don't at first get the grand outcomes that we're looking for. After all, how can we expect to accomplish Grand things without investing "Grand" time?

The Grand Canyon also reminds us that Grand accomplishments will always come with Grand

---

[1] Raney, W. "How Old Is The Grand Canyon?" *Geology.com*.

growing pains. The Canyon only became Grand after enduring years of constant erosion from the Colorado River, and if not for this perseverance in the face of pain the Canyon would never have been created. And so it is for us, if we too persevere through the promise of pain, as pieces of that which no longer serves us erodes away, we become poised to grow beyond our former station. This "letting go" can be difficult; after all, it is certainly far easier in the short-term to choose the easy way out and keep things as they are. However, to have what we have never had we must be willing to do what we have never done, and this will always require a sacrifice by giving up what we no longer need. In other words, to truly experience the beauty of today we must always remember that "what you don't have you don't need it now."[2]

For the Grand Canyon this sacrifice involved rock and sediment; for you and me, maybe it's old thought patterns or habits that only serve to hold us back. Perhaps it's friends, family, or colleagues that are discouraging us from growing, whether intentionally or intentionally. Maybe it's an old dream, or a current job. Maybe it's the feeling of comfort, security, and stability.

Leaving the security of the known for the unknown is simultaneously the scariest notion and the beginning of a fantastic adventure. For those who are

---

[2] U2. (2000). "Beautiful Day." *All That You Can't Leave Behind.* Santa Monica, CA: Island / Interscope.

no longer content with being "good" but rather wish to become Grand, we're hungry for something more. We're not comfortable being comfortable anymore, and to leave that comfort requires giving up what no longer serves us. We're operating from a higher level of standard. We can be upbeat about losing our former selves because with gratitude we experience joy in stepping into the next chapter of our lives.

The Positivity Papers is a collection of writings offering engagement, empowerment, and encouragement to individuals who are ready to step into the next chapter of their lives, while also serving as a valuable resource for motivated individuals seeking to be positive influences in the lives of others, but who might not know where to begin.

Our world is filled with conflicting influences and this book serves as a resource to cut through the noise of opposing forces in order to gain clarity, confidence, and courage to boldly step forward to make a positive impact for our own lives as well as for those around us.

RETHINKING POSITIVE THINKING

"Positive Thinking" is often viewed as the practice of wearing "rose-colored glasses," by pretending that everything is fine and dandy even when everything isn't fine and dandy. This so-called "willful blindness" keeps us in the dark even when "we could know, and should know—but don't know, because it makes us feel better not to know."[3] But can choosing to overlook reality really be considered "positive thinking?" Can the experience of a good lie really be a *good* thing? And can what we don't know—via genuine ignorance or willful blindness—actually hurt us?

The Positivity Papers addresses these issues by curating current research about the effects of positivity and negativity in everyday life, coupled with practical ideas for implementing these findings to benefit our work, relationships, and health. Along the way I'll also share my own personal adventures (and misadventures) in applying these tactics, along with relevant examples from our contemporary culture.

The ideas presented here will encourage you to think differently—about your life, about your work, about your relationships, and about your hopes and dreams. Truly, this book will challenge you to redefine your preconceived notions in order to learn new ways for working with reality—through thoughtful design coupled with purposeful actions—to facilitate positive experiences regardless of the circumstances.

MODALITIES OF POSITIVITY

Positivity is a broad topic with many modalities to explore—too many for the scope of this one volume—and so rather than attempting to cover

---

[3] Heffernan, M. (2004). *Willful Blindness: Why We Ignore the Obvious at Our Peril*. London, United Kingdom: Bloomsbury Publishing. p. 246

everything (an impossible task) this book aims to highlight certain key areas that are most relevant. How did I decide on the specific concentrations to present here? The answer is a practical one: Each issue in this volume was addressed to meet the immediate needs of Hashtag Positivity clients in 2018.

When an individual needed one-on-one coaching in a certain area of positivity, I wrote an article about it. When a corporate team invited me to train them in a certain area at their professional development day, I wrote about it. When an association needed me to address a specific topic at an annual conference, I wrote it down. When I was asked to speak at a college, I wrote down what we discussed and why it was important.

In this way, over the course of a year, an assortment of writings was collected addressing many issues within the positivity genre, and they are presented here, edited and reformatted, in the order in which they were written:

- **ISSUE 1**
  This article addresses the importance of carefully choosing what we focus on.

- **ISSUE 2**
  This selection addresses a strategy for finding the good in any situation.

- **ISSUE 3**
  This piece shares a strategy for making dreams come true.

- **ISSUE 4**
  This article offers encouragement for overcoming adversity.

- **ISSUE 5**
  This selection shares practices for making meaningful connections with others.

- **ISSUE 6**
  This piece discusses building a legacy.

- **ISSUE 7**
  This article shares ideas for staying encouraged in discouraging times.

- **ISSUE 8**
  This selection explores practices for fostering confidence.

- **ISSUE 9**
  This article shares strategies for increasing engagement.

- **ISSUE 10**
  This piece offers a formula for achieving a higher level of happiness.

- **ISSUE 11**
  This article poses three important questions to ask yourself before jumping into action.

- **ISSUE 12**
  This selection addresses the topic of positivity directly by exploring the latest research on the impacts of both positivity and negativity on our work, in our relationships, and for our health.

CONNECT

The Positivity Papers covers a lot of ground in just a few short pages, and the good news is that this doesn't have to be a solitary adventure. Remember, the Grand Canyon would not exist if not for the relationship it forged with the Colorado River. This demonstrates that our own Grand progress will rely on the meaningful connections that we foster with those around us. These relationships will involve your family, friends, colleagues, acquaintances, and perhaps even people you haven't even met yet—people who you will want to bring into your social circle to help enact personal and professional growth.

And remember, because you are investing your time in reading this book, I am now a part of your team, and you are now a part of mine. If you have any questions or comments, feel free to contact me directly by email at jonas@hashtagpositivity.com.

Together we will grow to become more than we could hope for apart. I'm excited to be on your team!

Photograph by Julie Neisch

Traversing The Grand Canyon
— May 16, 2018 —

The Positivity Papers: Volume 1

WHAT ARE YOU FOCUSING ON?

— Issue 1 —

When working with Hashtag Positivity clients one of the first things I ask them is where they are focusing their energy. We all have a desire to move forward confidently with our grand plans, but when we take an honest look at where we've been focusing our energy we often find that we've been missing the mark because we are simply focusing on the wrong things.

The good news is you can check to see where your focus is right now! In the chart on the next page there are a number of "positive" words hidden. The words are:

The Positivity Papers: Volume 1

1. ***Engage***
2. ***Empower***
3. ***Encourage***
4. ***Enjoyment***
5. ***Excellence***
6. ***Clarity***
7. ***Confidence***
8. ***Courage***
9. ***Kindness***
10. ***Empathy***

Take a moment or two now to see how many you can find.

```
S C R C V D E C L A R I T Y T B B E
I O R E O L D M E E N G A G E A J E
D N E E S K A O P X C T G U I L T N
X F G K N E O R U O C O A N G E R J
E I O O I C N X R B W E U W W R B O
M D P R E N O T A O T E L R P Y W Y
P E U G E B D U M T G I R L A E S M
A N B R E G T N R E L A G Z E G O E
T C N E O N R S E A N U N N K N E N
H E W E R F V E W S G T S C E T C T
Y M F D R X D Y T A S E C A E B D E
O J U P A L I E S U M Y K N R U I T
```

Did you find any?

Don't continue unless you found
at least a couple positive words.

Okay, I believe you.

Depending on how carefully you worked on this exercise you may have perhaps noticed that there are more words hidden in this puzzle than just the ones listed. The words hidden in this puzzle fall under two categories: "Positive" and "Negative." In fact, there is an equal number of positive words as negative words (20 in all) but if you did as instructed then chances are you found more positive words than negative words. The reason for this is that you were focused on looking for the positive rather than the negative.

WE GET WHAT WE LOOK FOR

We get what we focus on and we will see what we are looking for. This idea is similar to what scientists call a confirmation bias,[4] a tendency to interpret information according to our preexisting worldview—in this case the preconditioned desire to find what we are looking for. The very act of deciding to look for something makes the object of our desire more visible, like a yellow highlighter on a page.

---

[4] Heshmat, S. (2015, April 23).. "What Is Confirmation Bias?" PsychologyToday.com

Falling into extreme cases of confirmation bias can create problems (e.g. when we give unfounded meaning to the random and meaningless), however we can also use confirmation bias in healthy ways that develop and foster positivity. This can be especially helpful for those who are not naturally positive, or for those who have been "down in the dumps" lately.

FINAL THOUGHTS

It's not always easy to stay positive, especially when the unexpected happens, but by remembering that this is a daily practice rather than a one-and-done solution you can keep your expectations in perspective as you strive to focus on the things to be glad about.

The Positivity Papers: Volume 1

THE GLAD GAME

— Issue 2 —

*I*n my book *Are You P.O.S.I.T.I.V.E.? Rethinking Positive Thinking* I profile a list twenty different ways that people can exhibit negativity in their everyday lives. Two of the most common are *Complainers* and *Naysayers*. Nothing is ever good enough for Complainers, and whenever Naysayers find an opened window of opportunity they quickly draw the curtains!

To the eternal pessimist, everything is a problem worthy of lament; yet, to the eternal optimist, everything is an opportunity worthy of praise. In the 1913 book *Pollyanna* by Eleanor H. Porter, the author introduced a valuable strategy for maintaining positivity in the face of life's often-tumultuous surprises. The strategy is called The Glad Game:

> "The game was to just find something about everything to be glad about—no matter what 'twas."[5]

The goal of this game is to provide an opportunity for participants to gain a fresh perspective and let go of expectations, allowing them to see the positive side of circumstances—even ones that don't go as planned.

This is how it works:

1) Think of a <u>negative</u> circumstance (ex: "My car broke down")

2) Now add a <u>positive</u> prompt (ex: "I'm glad my car broke down, because now I'll get to…")

3) Lastly, finish the sentence with a positive outlook (ex: "…spend more time with my friend who will drive me to work.")

The idea is to allow the game to help you let go of expectations and see the good that every moment can bring if only you are open to it.

This notion of finding the good in everything is what philosophers call happiness resilience,[6] a phenomenon that returns us to a sense of normalcy even after a distressing situation. You can see a biological example of this at play when you consider what happens when you swim in a cool pool of water. At first the cold temperature comes as a shock to the

---

[5] Porter, E. H. (1913). *Pollyanna*. L.C. Page, 1913. p. 45
[6] Whitbourne, S. K. (2012), September 8). "Happiness: It's All About the Ending." PsychologyToday.com

body, yet over a relatively short period of time the body gradually adapts to the water.

FINAL THOUGHTS

It's not always easy to stay positive, especially when the unexpected happens, but by remembering that this is a daily practice rather than a one-and-done solution you can keep your expectations in perspective as you strive to focus on the things to be glad about. What are YOU focusing on?

MAKE YOUR IDEAS A REALITY

— Issue 3 —

We all have an idea, a dream, or a goal that we'd like to accomplish, but for many these ideas, dreams, and goals remain visionless thoughts never to see the light of day. Writer and three-time Pulitzer Prize winner Carl Sandburg reminds us that "nothing happens but first a dream," which is certainly true. Dreaming allows us to see things that others can't see—to see things not for how they are and have always been, but for how they could be.

A common complaint about dreamers, though, is that they spend too much time up in the clouds, but dreamers know that that's how to get the really good view! Instead of having an ant's-eye views they climb high to get an eagle's-eye view! Yet the same thing that serves dreamers well can also be a drawback if they're not careful. After all, what's the use of seeing the bigger picture if we're not able to identify and articulate the details to make that dream a reality? In other words, a dream without vision has no chance of ever becoming a reality

Martin Luther King Jr. reminds us of this problem when he said: "The difference between a dreamer and a visionary is that a dreamer has his eyes closed and a visionary has his eyes open." In this way we can understand that a dreamer who's become a visionary is one who comes down from the clouds, identifies the details to make a dream a reality, and is able to articulate the dream in tandem with the details so that other can see the clear pathway for success. And therein rests the keyword: clear. To turn an idea into reality we need clarity.

In July of 2017 I climbed Mount Washington for the first time and as I approached the final stretch to the summit I became enveloped in clouds. This became a safety concern because I was relying on the queue of cairns to guide me to the top! Whenever I stumbled upon each marker I was unable to see the next one, leaving me to guess and hope I was headed in the right direction rather than over the side of the mountain. But there were random and fleeting moments of amazing clarity that let me know I was on the right path. The wind would blow, the clouds would clear out, and I'd clearly see the path ahead of me—with the trail of markers laid out and the hundreds of other hikers that I didn't even know were there! These moments wouldn't last long before the clouds would return, but they offered vision and direction for making it to the top. Plus, it was also comforting to know that there were so many other people around me on the same path!

Clarity is the magic ingredient that can turn a mere dream into a vision and vision into reality. Yet, without clarity, we find ourselves irritable and dissatisfied, clouding our mind from seeing what is right in front of us, which is a world of possibilities!

So the question becomes, how do we develop more clarity? Or perhaps a better question, what causes a lack of clarity? Because if we know and understand what causes a lack of clarity—and then we work to eliminate those causes—then we won't have to seek clarity at all because it will naturally come find us!

I believe a major cause of a lack of clarity is disorganization, and our lives become disorganized:

- When we aren't clear on our values.

- When we avoid responsibility and focus on the things that we think are important all the while avoiding the things that are really important.

- When we blindly go through our days, stuck in a repetitive cycle that doesn't stop to reflect on what or why we're doing all the things that we do.

- When we aren't clear on our values, when we have "backwards" responsibilities, and when we don't take moments of self-reflection we will forever stay "lost in the clouds."

GET ORGANIZED

To gain more clarity we can begin by organizing our lives in three ways:

1. **Examine Your Values**

    What are they? What's important to you? Are you currently living according to your values? Why or why not? What can you do today to better match your actions to your values?

2. **Identify Your Responsibilities**

    What have you been avoiding but need to take full charge of? What have you been accepting responsibility for but truly have no control over? Whatever your truly responsibilities are, they are a part of your action plan towards achieving success.

3. **Reflect On Your Habits**

    We will never change our lives for the better until we change something that we do every day. What is one new habit that you can implement starting today to move you closer to achieving you dreams and goals? In a similar way, what is one habit that you need to give up in order to go up? What are you willing to sacrifice?

Final Thoughts

If we follow through with these three simple items—Values,[7] Responsibilities,[8] and Habits—we'll unclutter our lives to see all the obstacles in our way and gain a clear path to the mountaintop of our success!

---

[7] hashtagpositivity.com/vlog/value
[8] hashtagpositivity.com/vlog/responsibility

The Positivity Papers: Volume 1

HOW TO OVERCOME ADVERSITY

— Issue 4 —

When I was fourteen years old I was invited to perform a magic act at my high school talent show. This was my first opportunity to perform in front of the entire school and I was eager to impress them, so I created a magic demonstration that was sure to amaze; a piece I menacingly entitled *Acid Roulette*.

Imagine the scene: Six test tubes each filled with water except for one, which instead contained hydrochloric acid. Colorless and odorless, the acid looked and smelled just like water, but certainly didn't *taste* like water. The idea was I'd be blindfolded as a member of the audience mixed up the test tubes, and then I would blindly drink from each of them leaving only the test tube with the acid untouched. That was the idea. (The ridiculous, absurd idea!)

On the night of the talent show everything went perfectly according to plan, until something went wrong. The first test tube I drank from *had the acid*! This was no joke! I immediately spit it out tore off the blindfold and ran off the stage! The audience, not thinking I'd actually use *real* acid, thought that it was a joke and they proceeded to just laugh and laugh as I continued running around yelling for help.

**Mere Moments Before Drinking Acid
— May 27, 1998 —**

During the ensuing hospital stay I had plenty of time to reflect on where I went wrong. Even though I had practiced the stunt, in rehearsal I didn't actually use real acid (after all, why practice something that you can only afford to fail once?) So in rehearsal I instead used seltzer, and it worked fine—most of the time. Sometimes I drank the seltzer by mistake, but as the night of the talent show got closer and closer I was running out of time and was relying on this stunt to be the big closure of my act, so I decided that it just *needed* to work, so I just put on a "positive attitude" about the whole thing and went for it. Unfortunately this "positive attitude" ignored the reality of my circumstances—it ignored the fact that it was not a good idea!

While few people have actually attempted such an absurd stunt, as fallible beings we at times approach our work in a similar way, with a woeful lack of preparation and forethought.

We all have dreams and goals, but even when we make the best-made plans with the best intentions that alone doesn't ensure success. Despite our efforts not everything is in our control, so what do we do? Do we just hope and pray (like I did with the acid incident)? Do we give up at the first sign of adversity? Or do we perhaps not even try at all for fear of looking like a fool or a failure (or both!)?

I've been practicing magic now for over two decades and what I've come to understand is that a successful magic performance has far less to do with sleight of hand and misdirection, and instead has much more to do with being an expert in managing surprises. The ability to adapt to an ever-changing environment where anything and everything could go wrong (and usually does!) and yet still be able arrive at a positive result is what separates the amateurs from the pros. And *that*, my friends, is the *real* magic.

STRATEGY

Like any good magic trick, the question becomes: *"How is this possible?!"* How is it possible to have a positive outcome even when circumstances don't align with our plans? One of the strategies that magicians use to manage results is to practice our mistakes. It perhaps sounds counterintuitive, right? After all, by definition mistakes are things that *shouldn't* happen, so why focus any amount of energy on getting better at doing the very things that we *don't* want to have happen? Diving deeper into this same line of thinking, however, gives us the answer.

Magic coaches tell us that we should analyze every possible way that something could go wrong, and then practice our magic tricks as if we've made those mistakes. By practicing our mistakes before we've even made them, when things do eventually go wrong we already know what to do to have a successful outcome because we've already thought about it—we've already practiced it and are experts at making those mistakes work to our advantage.

APPLICATION

One of my mentors once recounted the time a flight he was on had a difficult landing: just as the plane touched down a sudden wind jolted the plane crooked and the pilot immediately brought the plane back up into the air to circle back again for a safer landing. My mentor was amazed at the pilot's quick action and as he departed the plane he stopped to thank him for getting everyone down safely, then asked how he had made such a quick decision. The pilot responded that he had already made that decision twenty years earlier. As a young pilot he had thought about all the things that could go wrong and decided that when anything should go wrong with a landing he should immediately get the plane back into the air. The success of that challenging landing was decided years earlier because the pilot had already analyzed what could go wrong and rehearsed every best response in his mind.

While I've never piloted a plane, I have had my fair share of plane rides, and even jumped out of a couple of them. I'm happy to say that this strategy of analyzing every possible outcome has helped to keep me alive every time (so far). I suspect this is mostly because I know myself enough to strap myself to someone who has made that jump thousands of times before. But that's a lesson for another day.

FINAL THOUGHTS

We will never truly know how things will work out, but by analyzing all the possible outcomes there's a good chance we'll be well prepared, come what may, to steer the circumstances in our favor to achieve positive results.

3 STEPS FOR FOSTERING EFFECTIVE CONNECTIONS
The Real Secrets of Magic

— ISSUE 5 —

*O*ne of my favorite moments as a magician happened during the spring of 2009. I was contracted to tour all the senior centers in Springfield, MA with my magic act and during one of the stops I was met with a most unfortunate circumstance. Everyone was playing bingo.

If there's one thing I've learned as a performer it's that no one wants to be interrupted from what they're doing to watch a magic show. Especially senior citizens playing bingo! After explaining that I had been booked to present that day a woman in the back of the room gave me a stern stare and a scowl. Her only question was, "How long is your show going to take?"

"It depends," I replied. "If everyone is enjoying themselves and participating then the show can go as long as an hour, but if there's not as much participation then it will probably be over in about 40 minutes or so."

Her response wasn't very reassuring: "It will be a short show."

Regardless of the circumstances and the criticism, I boldly stepped forward and performed giving everyone my best effort. To be sure, there were a number of folks there that were interested in my presentation and I quickly aligned myself with those allies, but I kept a close eye on that woman in the back.

It was about halfway through the performance that I noticed her expression begin to change. Where once there was a scowl there appeared a smile, and where once there was scorn there was now laughter. By the end of the show this same woman who had wanted nothing to do with me actually willingly volunteered to participate in the finale!

As I was making my rounds after the show thanking everyone for having me, the woman pulled me aside and shared with me one of the best compliments I have ever received. She said, "Jonas, I don't like magicians, but I like you!"

THE SECRET OF MAGIC
I've been practicing magic for over twenty years and perhaps the number one question I'm asked is *"How'd*

you do it?" The honest answer is never what people think. What I've come to understand is that what makes for a successful magic show has less to do with sleight of hand, smoke and mirrors, and instead has much more to do with making meaningful connections with others. Every time I walk out on stage in a theatre, or ballroom, or up to the front of a conference room, I'm walking into a situation where I have to work with people that I've never met, and yet I still have to arrive at a positive outcome.

Perhaps the best encouragement I've found in this regard comes from the words attributed to President Theodore Roosevelt:

> "The most important single ingredient in the formula of success is knowing how to get along with people."

In other words, I could be the greatest magician in the world *technically*, but if I haven't learned how to demonstrate genuine care and mutual respect for others then no one's going to care one way or another whether I can find their playing card!

The real secret to magic, and the real challenge of any salesperson, customer service rep, manger, spouse, sibling, and so forth, is learning how to make meaningful connections so we can work with one another positively and effectively. This is challenging for many, however, because so many of us simply don't give any thought to increasing our capacity for making meaningful connections, either because we don't think of it as a skill that can be honed, or because we don't think of it as important. And because so many of us simply don't think of it, it stays off of our radar, unaware that we could be achieving so much more if only we invest effort in this area.

SHIFT IN FOCUS
If you're interested in achieving more and would like to learn to connect more effectively and meaningfully with others, then a good place to start is by making a shift in your focus. Communication tends to be about you—it's about what you have to say and how you say it. Connecting, on the other hand, is about others—it's about relating to others on common ground where beliefs, values, and goals intersect. This should be an easy task for folks who work for the same organization, are in the same department, are members of the same family, and so forth—seeing as they have an obvious common connector—yet even in these circumstances trouble can arise, when disagreements in direction, values, and ethics come up.

To overcome such issues here are three simple steps that you can use to increase your capacity for connecting with others:

1. Be Likeable
There is a fine line between seeking likability to achieve a worthy cause and seeking likability to feed "approval addiction," but with the right intentions

likeability can be a powerful tool for connecting with others. Being likeable in this context means demonstrating genuine care and respect for others. This is perhaps the most influential factor in working with others. Simply put, if people like you they will listen to you, and if they don't then they won't. The woman from the story at the beginning of this article wanted nothing to do with me until I was able to make myself likeable, and once I was able to do that it opened the door for a positive experience.

How do we demonstrate care and respect to foster likeability? One way is by asking questions.

2. Ask Questions

Asking people questions is not only a great way to get to know them—and therefore enabling you to better identify common ground—but it also communicates that you are genuinely interested in them. This involves honestly listening to the answers you receive and it also involves asking some self-reflection questions. Do you feel what they feel? Do you see what they see? Do you know what they know? Do you want what they want? Asking questions of this quality puts you in the mindset of seeking to serve rather than to be served.

Once we have the answers to our questions we can put them to use with humility.

3. Be Humble

Humility is often associated with weakness, however it's properly viewed as a strength for those confident in their abilities. This view of humility is inspired by the British poet and journalist Alan Ross who suggests that humility means knowing and using our strengths for the benefit of others on behalf of a higher purpose. In all of my magic performances the emphasis is never on me; rather, it's always on the audience. In fact, there are many segments in my act that are designed to empower the audience to allow them to make the magic happen *themselves*! Humble leaders don't think less of themselves; rather, they simply choose instead to consider the needs of others in fulfilling a worthy cause. When we make others look good by facilitating opportunities for their best selves to shine, not only do we become much more likable, but we also gain friends and influence. This is the real secret of magic!

FINAL THOUGHTS

In the end, people will not always remember what we say and they will not always remember what we do, but they will always *always* remember how we made them feel. If we seek to be kind, caring, and humble, then the results will be opportunities to make meaningful connections with others.

Perhaps an effective summary of these ideas is found in the *101% Principle*, which suggests that we find the 1% that we have in common, then give that our 100% effort. When we work to connect with others in this way, I assure you, the results will be magical!

WHAT'S YOUR LEGACY?

— Issue 6 —

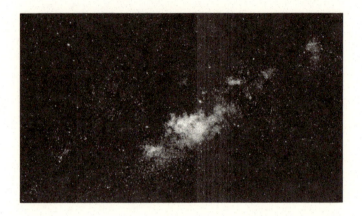

*I*t was night when I arrived, but even in the darkness I recognized the house. It was almost as if I had been there before. Knew I was in the right place when I caught a glimpse of Stephanie and a couple other folks coming out of the house. Didn't want her to see me just yet, in case there was a reason she had stayed away for eleven years, so I hid inside a nearby van, crouching down in the backseat. This proved to be a terrible place to hide, because Stephanie and her friends got into the van too! Thankfully they stayed up front and didn't see me crouching quietly in the back.

My heart was pounding. Between the beats I could hear what they were talking about. They were talking about me! Stephanie told her friends that she loves me, and that she knows how much I loved her, but she's surprised I didn't come looking for her when she left. Hearing this, I decided it was time to speak up.

"They told me you were dead." Everyone was startled when they heard my voice. They looked back just in time to see me coming up from behind the back seat. When our eyes met Stephanie smiled the smile I know well. It was beautiful, what more could I say?

"They even had a body to show me at your funeral!" I continued, as I started making my way to the middle of the van.

"That's not how it works," Stephanie replied, as she began making her way to meet me in the middle. "Yeah, it was my body, but it wasn't me. I just went somewhere else. I'm still around; there's lots of work to do here."

"I'm happy to know you're still around," I said just as we were finally close enough to touch. Our eyes locked, just as they always had, as if no years had kept them apart.

Then I leaned in. She leaned in too. For the first time in eleven years our lips embraced. Everything came back! All at once! The sensation was such a shock to my Being that it instantly zapped me awake!

It was still early so I turned over and tried to fall back asleep to be with Stephanie again. It had been a long and fast eleven years, and even though it was just a dream I wanted to live in the fantasy again, even if only for a little while. But I couldn't sleep, because I didn't really want it. Now that I'm awake (now that my eyes and heart are opened) they won't be shut. Knowing what I now know (knowing again, remembering what I knew, re-cognizing the Truth) I don't want to fall asleep again. We have lots of work to do, work that we couldn't do before.

LESSONS FROM GRIEF

I don't talk much anymore about my experience with grief in the years following Stephanie's sudden and unexpected death just a week after we became engaged to be married. This is partially because I've talked and written and thought and lived it enough that I'm ready for a new story, but certainly it's also because the pain is now gone. To be sure, I still think about her every day—not a day goes by that the thought of her doesn't cross my mind—yet time has been a good medicine.

What also helped the healing process was an important question that began ruminating about eight years ago. What if the roles were reversed? What if I had died instead? What would Stephanie say about me? What would anyone say about me? This lead to a similar yet profoundly different question: What if I died today? What legacy would my actions while I was here leave behind?

In the early years since Stephanie's passing I didn't handle grief very well. I had become a person that I didn't recognize, doing things that my former self would never have dreamed of doing. But this question of legacy began reframing my attitude and approach towards life, and this new approach forced me to take a critical look at my actions.

Thomas J. Watson, IBM's first CEO (and the namesake of the company's question and answer machine) once said: "Nothing so conclusively proves a man's ability to lead others as what he does from day to day to lead himself." Put another way: Do we have the strength of character to do the right thing even when doing the wrong thing would be far easier?

WHAT'S YOUR LEGACY?

If we could spend a day together to talk about your passions—your natural talents, learned skills, and causes that stir your spirit—with only one day we'd only be able to scratch the surface of what it can take to develop and foster our capacity for self-leadership. It's for this reason that I suggest here just one big idea, because keeping this one idea in mind as you grow through life will enable you to make the really tough decisions when they come, while at the same time making the rest of life simply more enjoyable.

The big idea is this: At the end of your life people will summarize your life in one sentence. Choose your sentence now. Choose the legacy you want to leave others and then live today and every day in such a way that your influence continues to positively impact others even long after you're gone.

One of my mentor's, John C. Maxwell, puts it another way. He asks: "What kind of a bridge are you building for those who follow?" Answering this question gives clarity and vision for our day-to-day decision-making, because what we do every day is what decides our legacy for us. Deciding on the bridge that we build is a decision that's fully within our control. We do get to decide how we live. "We decide which is right and which is an illusion."[9]

So, how about it? What do you want your legacy to be? Why is this important to you? If you don't know what you want your legacy to be, then perhaps a good question to get you started is this: What will your legacy be if you died today? If you don't like the answer to this pointed question, what will it take to change that?

FINAL THOUGHTS

As we grow through life our thoughts about legacy will often change, continually refining and becoming ever clearer as we move forward. Whatever you decide, as you continue to move forward I encourage you to keep this question in mind: Will your actions today leave a positive legacy when you're gone?

---

[9] The Moody Blues. (1967). "Late Lament." *Days of Future Passed*. London, United Kingdom: Deram.

2 STRATEGIES TO HELP YOU STAY ENCOURAGED

— ISSUE 7 —

"Those who are lifting the world upward and onward are those who encourage more than criticize."

— ELIZABETH HARRISON

*H*as this ever happened to you? You find yourself inspired, yet wholly unmotivated to actually put such inspiration into action? People are endowed with passions—the intersection of their natural talents and burning interests—and are called to share those unique gifts with he world; yet, for many, those passions go unused. What gives?

As far as I can tell there are two primary stumbling stones that can hold anyone back: 1) Being discouraged by others, and 2) being discouraged by past disappointment. Some of the most dangerous people in our lives are those well-meaning (or *not* so well-meaning) loved ones who discourage us from doing what we really need to do, and instead settle for average and less than we were born for. In a similar way, putting ourselves out there and getting burned can also be a painful source of discouragement, keeping us from pursing real and lasting happiness.

Are You A Viewer, Or A Participant?

For the past eighteen years I've served as a youth leadership counselor for the Massachusetts American Legion and Auxiliary Boy's and Girls' State Programs. One of the many roles I've served with this organization includes that of choir director (they've never heard me sing so they didn't know any better!) During the 2017 season I was leading the choir during their final performance at the big gala celebration. As they walked off the stage I gave them a big thumbs up saying, "Great job!" Just as I said this one student looked me in the eyes and said, "Don't lie!"

I don't think this student was trying to be humble; rather, I think she was perhaps looking at the situation with different eyes (or ears). Admittedly, their performance wasn't their best work. It wasn't terrible, but it wasn't their best work. So no, their *performance* wasn't great, but that wasn't what I was encouraging. You see, there were over 600 students at the program that week, and out of those participants less than 20 stepped up to join the choir. Less than 20 had the guts to step up in front of over 600 of their peers to sing their heart out.

Perhaps what I most appreciated about the choir that week was that most of them didn't have any formal music training, yet they decided to get the most out of their experience with the program by trying something new, and *that's* what I was congratulating them on and *that's* why I was encouraging them. Meanwhile, there were several students who didn't have the courage to step up who actually *did* have musical training, but they chose instead to take life sitting down.

SHOW UP TO THE ARENA

Think about this: Olympic Gold Medals don't go to the best athletes in the world; rather, they go to the best athletes that actually show up to the arena. The world doesn't need passive viewers of life who seek the illusion of happiness through security and the status quo; the world doesn't need people avoiding scrapped knees, humbled pride, and bruised egos. Rather, what the world needs are people who become truly alive, who seek true and solid happiness by becoming active participants with life; what the world needs are people who aren't afraid of scrapping their knees, humbling their pride, and bruising their ego every now and again.

Many are inspired to live an engaged life, yet few are motivated to actually follow through. Whether discouraged by others or by past disappointment, one of the greatest tragedies of life is when people fail to pursue their passions.

PRACTICES TO STAY ENCOURAGED

In my book *Are You P.O.S.I.T.I.V.E.?: Rethinking Positive Thinking*,[10] I share an eight-step process for developing and fostering positivity to enjoy and excel in life at work, home, and beyond. For the purposes of this article, here are a couple quick practices that you can implement starting today to stay encouraged:

1. When encountering a discourager, consider:

What's their authority on the subject?

Does this person have personal experience with what you're trying to do? Or did they just hear about an experience from someone else? What were the circumstances like? Everyone and every situation is different. As the ancient Greek philosopher Heraclitus reminds us, "No man ever steps in the same river twice, for it's not the same river and he's not the same man." Everything is in flow so just because someone had a negative experience that doesn't mean that you will too. In a similar way, just because someone has a

---

[10] Cain, J. I. (2018). *Are You P.O.S.I.T.I.V.E.? Rethinking Positive Thinking*. Boston, MA: Hashtag Positivity.

positive experience that doesn't mean that you will have that same experience.

Some people fail because they didn't really want it to work out. Perhaps they were doing it out of obligation or trying to make someone else happy. Some people fail because they didn't try hard enough. Maybe out of lack of knowledge, skills, or desire. Yet others fail because of circumstances completely outside of their control, and so no matter how hard they would have tried it just would never have worked out. Notice, though, that none of this has anything to do with you.

What do they stand to lose if you succeed?

Discouragers often try to hold others back because they believe they stand to lose if others win. This can either be a real or imagined worry for them. Perhaps they want to succeed in that area, and so they see you as a threat, or perhaps they feel inadequate to succeed, and to see others grow in life is viewed as a threat to their ego. In either case, their concerns have nothing to do with you.

What do they stand to gain if you lose?

This is another way of asking the last question, but puts the emphasis in the other direction. If someone sees you as a threat to their own success or as a threat to their ego, if you lose, what benefit will it be to them? Either way, it has nothing to do with you.

2. When you find yourself in a situation where you're discouraged by past disappointments, consider these questions:

Why do you want to do what you're considering?

Knowing the real reason for why you want to do something can be very empowering. Oftentimes we go through life with vague ideas, simply accepting what life gives us; yet by taking a step back and getting clear on our values and priorities we become empowered. And when we have a compelling enough reason for taking a course of action we become much more inclined to pursue it, even in the face of risks.

What do you stand to gain if you succeed?

This question supports the last question. When what you stand to gain by stepping up is greater than the cost of staying down, you become compelled into action.

What do you stand to lose if you don't try?

This question helps you to gain even more clarity in understanding your "why." When what you stand to *lose* by not taking action is of greater consequence than the cost of trying (even if you fail), you become encouraged to jump into action.

How are your past situations similar or dissimilar to your current situation?

Just as Heraclitus reminded us earlier, everything is in flow, and therefore nothing is ever the same and no two situations are alike. Just because you may have had a negative experience that doesn't mean that you will continue to always have negative experiences. In a similar way, just because you may have had a positive experience that doesn't mean that you will continue to have those same experiences. Like the ocean tides, everything is in flow. Remembering this will provide encouragement to stand back up from pain. In other words, perhaps this is good mantra to remember: "I'm never down. I'm either up or getting up!"

EVERYTHING IS IN FLOW

I know full well that past disappointments can be discouraging. I've been engaged twice and married once, and between experiencing the death of my fiancée and the divorce from my wife I can say with authority that the pain of lost love can be highly discouraging. Yet I also recognize that these experiences are just that: experiences. And when we move forward from experiences we understand that they are ever-changing, because nothing remains the same. Over the years love has been likened to a river by poets and songwriters, but it's never the same river.

In the face of such circumstances we can ask ourselves these questions: Do we want to avoid loving relationships because we can't control the actions of others, so why bother putting trust in them? Do we want to avoid loving relationships because the promise of human life is death, so why bother putting trust in someone who's just going to eventually die? Or do we choose instead to recognize that everything is in flow, and that the next potential partner has nothing to do with the people from our past?

Final Thoughts

Many are inspired, yet few are motivated. This is a call for encouragement because what the world needs is people to become truly alive by sharing their passions with the world. If the bug of inspiration has ever bitten you, then you know how wonderful it can be. The big question is, what are you doing about it? What first steps have you taken? What skills or knowledge do you need pick up along the way to go the distance? Whatever your ambition, if it's something that will make your heart sing and bring more enjoyment to the world, then I encourage you to move forward with it!

3 EMPOWERMENT PRACTICES TO INCREASE CONFIDENCE

— ISSUE 8 —

*"What can I learn today so that tomorrow
I will be well poised to not just be a day older
but a day wiser too?"*

— JONAS CAIN

*I*t's been said that the greatest responsibility of a leader is to empower their followers. But what exactly does it mean to "empower?" The dictionary defines empowerment as the authority and power to do something. With this in mind, I'd suggest that the responsibility of empowerment extends not just to others but to the self as well. After all, how can we possibility expect to give to others what we ourselves don't already possess? Self-empowerment, therefore, is a prerequisite to empowering others.

EMPOWERMENT PRACTICES

In my book *Are You P.O.S.I.T.I.V.E.? Rethinking Positive Thinking*,[11] I share an eight-step process for developing and fostering positivity to experience more enjoyment and excellence in life. Three of these practices are relevant to our discussion on empowerment and so I will share them here so you can begin implementing today for your own personal empowerment:

1. Stimulate Your Passions

Here passion is defined as the intersection of our talents and our interests. That is, the cross-section of the things that we can do better than most people with little or no effort, and the things that we think about even when we should be thinking about other things. When we combine these two things, Bippity Boppity Boo, we find passion.

Experts often say that we should focus on our passions because it helps us become most engaged in our work, however *stimulating* our passions takes us a step further because it highlights the gap between what we want to do and what we're currently capable of doing.

It's kind of like the gap between a train and a station platform: if we're not aware of the gap then we could end up falling and missing the train! In a similar

---

[11] Cain, J. I. (2018). *Are You P.O.S.I.T.I.V.E.? Rethinking Positive Thinking*. Boston, MA: Hashtag Positivity.

way, if we aren't aware of our skills and knowledge gap then we can end up missing the train of life and never get to where we want to go with our lives.

In his book *High Performance Habits*, personal growth expert Brendon Burchard talks about this same idea. He says:

> "A Super Bowl-winning quarterback doesn't just know how to throw a ball. He has had to master mental toughness, nutrition, self-discipline, contract negotiations, brand building, and so on. Someone who reaches high performance in any career must have competence in many of the areas that touch that career."[12]

There's a difference between someone who knows how to throw a ball and someone who celebrates the success of a Super Bowl Win. And that difference is a one person came down out of the clouds, stimulated their passions, and did everything they needed to turn the dream into a vision.

What's your passion? What skills and knowledge touch that passion? Empower yourself today and every day by stimulating your passions.

2. Identify Your Responsibilities

Winston Churchill once said that the price of greatness is responsibility. One source of empowerment, then, is to identify our responsibilities. In a world where

---

[12] Burchard, B. (2017). *High Performance Habits*. Carlsbad, CA: Hay House. p. 15

many avoid responsibility by doing just the bare minimum to get by, the path of responsibility is one where we'll perhaps find few travel companions, yet it's one well worth the effort.

An important thing to keep in mind here is that we sometimes hold ourselves accountable for things that we truly have no control over. There's a difference between the things that we can change and the things that we need to just let go of. Our task, then, is to identify what we can control so that we are able to recognize our true responsibilities.

To get start, consider these questions:

a) What can you control?

b) What responsibilities do you have to yourself?

c) If you have a family (parents, spouse, children...) what are your responsibilities to them?

d) If you live in a community, what is your responsibility as a neighbor?

e) If you have a job, what is your responsibility to your employer, co-workers, and customers?

f) If you are a member of the human race, and a citizen of this Earth, what are your responsibilities to the world?

The concept of responsibility is simple yet it can at times be challenging to put into practice, at least in the beginning. It's safe to say that most everyone wants to change the world for the better; it's just that not everyone is willing to change themselves. By identifying our responsibilities we'll become empowered to experience positive growth because it cuts through the distracting noise of everyday life, highlighting a clear path for action.

The important thing to remember is to take that first step. There are only so many hours in the day. Saying NO to things that you aren't responsible for frees up your schedule to say YES to the things that are your responsible. Empower yourself today by identifying your responsibilities.

3. Invest in Worthy Guides

In 2015 I went skydiving for the first time. I wouldn't particularly call myself a daredevil; rather, I simply put my trust in those who are masters of their craft. I didn't dive into the sky alone. Rather, I dove into the sky with the security of being strapped to someone who had made that same jump literally thousands of times. The ancient Greek stoic philosopher Epictetus, in the book *Enchiridion*, is quoted as saying:

> "One of the best ways to elevate your character immediately is to find worthy role models to emulate."

Consider that successful sport teams never go it alone; rather, they always have a coach to help show them the way. These coaches are people who have prior knowledge and experience that they use to offer advice and encouragement. They've gone that way before and can offer a welcomed perspective of things to look for, things to avoid, and things to try along the journey. Just as a sports team would never go into a game without a coach, it would be just as silly for you or I to try to go it alone in the game of life when there are worthy coaches, guides, and mentors available to us.

That's the power of a worthy guide. They can take us to the edge and guide us safely through the thrill of positive growth and development. They show us the way, tell us what tools and skills we'll need, and advise use when to jump and when to hold back. Empower yourself today by investing in worthy guides.

FINAL THOUGHTS

Empowerment gives us the confidence and motivation to jump into action with our grand plans, while a lack of empowerment holds us back. Ultimately there are three kinds of people when it comes to disempowerment:

1. Those who don't know what they would like to do. In other words, they are confused.

2. Those who know what they want to do, but don't do it. In other words, they are frustrated

3. Those who know what they want to do, and do it. In other words, they are fulfilled.

If lately you've been feeling unmotivated, unconfident, and unfulfilled, then there's no need to be. Try the three simple empowerment practices shared here to increase your empowered and see what they can do for you.

THE KEY TO ENGAGEMENT

— Issue 9 —

*T*here's an often-quoted mantra that says: "No matter how you feel, get up, dress up, and show up."[13] This is a valuable sentiment that should not to be taken lightly. According to a worldwide Gallup study of 142 countries, only 13% of workers are actively engaged in their work.[14] This means that 87% of the workforce isn't in the game to win—they're simply in the game to not lose! Rather than making an honest effort to consciously contribute in a positive way to their companies and organizations, these workers are more interested in doing just enough to keep their jobs and not get fired.

---

[13] Attributed to author Regina Brett.
[14] Crabtree, S. (2013). "Worldwide, 13% of Employees Are Engaged at Work." Gallup.com

Whether this describes you or the people on your team, "no matter how you feel, get up, dress up, and show up" is a good way to start—however there's more to "showing up" than simply looking the part and being physically present. If that's all we do then it's as effective putting a suit on a mannequin! Engagement—being fully present and committed to excellence—requires more.

When I was a student at Salem State University one of my favorite professors was Mandy Lobraico, a true communicator who highlighted the potential power of engagement. In her classes she made sure that every question was answered completely and she wouldn't test us on what she taught until she was sure that we understood the material. This approach to education guaranteed success, so long as you showed up each day and engaged in each lesson. Failure simply was not possible so long as you were engaged. Of course, some students still failed her course, because some students didn't bother showing up! Other students showed up but sat in the back of the room and tuned out. They may have dressed up and showed up, but they weren't *really* there because they lacked engagement.

GAUGING ENGAGEMENT

If you're looking to increase your level of engagement then it helps to develop awareness—both for when you are and when you are not engaged. To help with this, the author Eckhart Tolle promotes what he calls *modalities of awakened doing.*[15] The concept is simple: whatever it is you do, seek to do it with enthusiasm, enjoyment, or acceptance. The ultimate goal is to be enthusiastic, but enjoyment is still, well, enjoyable! But at the very least, we must be able to accept what we are doing.

Part of the allure of enthusiasm is that when we have it, we no longer need motivation, because when we're enthusiastic about our work we become naturally motivated, fully engaged, confident in ourselves and our abilities.

Enjoyment has it's own benefits too. I still recall the thrill I felt on September 9, 2017 when I was able to execute, for the first time ever, a chin-up! It was an incredible moment created by a year and a half of weightlifting to build up strength, and running upwards of 8 miles a day to lose weight. I was not always enthusiastic about the process, yet I continue to find enjoyment in knowing that every day I'm doing the work necessary to enact positive changes.

Acceptance may not be the most exciting of the three modalities, but it does have its place. Anything worthwhile will require an honest effort, and sometimes that means doing things that we'd rather not experience. If we're truly committed and truly

---

[15] Tolle, E. (2006). *A New Earth*. Westminster, United Kingdom: Penguin Books. p. 310

engaged in the process, then acceptance can see us through.

You will know that you're sincerely engaged in your work and in your life when you can do everything with genuine enthusiasm, enjoyment, or acceptance. In a similar way, you will know that you are disengaged and have gone the wrong way if for too many days, or weeks, or months in a row you can't even accept what you're doing. Perhaps it means you've been lying to yourself. Maybe you've accepted someone else's dream. Maybe you're afraid to do what you really want to do in life, discouraged by others or by past disappointment. Or perhaps you just don't know what it is you really want to do. Whatever the case may be, if you don't have enthusiasm, enjoyment, or acceptance, then it's a clear sign that it's time to find another way.

ENGAGEMENT PRACTICES

One my favorite strategies for thinking, being, and staying positive is simple yet easy to implement immediately to foster and develop engagement.

This strategy employs your passions, which we'll define as the intersection of your talents and your interests. We'll define your talents as the things that you can do better than most people with little or no effort, and your interests as the things that you think about even when you should be thinking about something else. Experts suggest that you should focus on your passions because it gets you engaged in your work. While this is true, it also stops too soon. Focusing on your passions may get you into the game, but to get stay in the game you'll need to take it a step further, and that's where *stimulating your passions* comes into play.

By stimulating your passions the process highlights any gaps between what you want to do and what you're currently able to do. It fills in your "to do list" with things that lie beyond your natural interests and natural talents, recognizing that you'll need to gain skills and knowledge that touch your passion. Stimulating your passions enables you to grow beyond where you currently are, closing any and all gaps before they ever have a chance to hold you back.

> "The most successful people start with a dominant talent and then add skills, knowledge and practice into the mix."[16]

The practice of stimulating your passions relieves the tension between contentment and excellence, ensuring that you remain an active participant in all that you do.

FINAL THOUGHTS

Remember, approximately 7 out of 8 of the workers today have actively "checked out," and are more interested in doing just enough to get by than

---

[16] Tardanico, S. (2011, April 27) "Stop Worrying About Your Weaknesses. Focus on Your Strengths." Forbes.com

contributing in a positive way to their companies, communities, and beyond. The good news is that if this describes you or your team for too many days, weeks, or months in a row (or years in a row!) then you're not alone. The even better news is that there are tangible action steps that you can employ to do something about it:

1. Get up, dress up, and show up.
2. Recognize when you have (and don't have) enthusiasm, enjoyment, and acceptance.
3. Stimulate your passions.

If you're been struggling with engagement lately, keep these principles and practices in mind. It's easy to stay engaged when the tides are in your favor; it's another matter when the tides go against you. Preparing yourself now for the storms of life will ensure consistent engagement regardless of circumstances.

The Positivity Papers: Volume 1

HOW TO EXPERIENCE A HIGHER LEVEL OF HAPPINESS

— Issue 10 —

Photograph by Julie Neisch

As a magician I've always been on the lookout for the greatest magic trick of all. When I was younger I thought it would have something to do with mastering sleight of hand or using smoke and mirrors, but what I eventually came to understand is that the greatest magic of all has nothing to do with tricks and instead has more to do with something much more valuable.

Before I share this idea I'll give you some context for how I stumbled upon this concept:

> Think of the last time you were disrupted by something outside of your control. For example, it might be a colleague, spouse, or friend who did something unexpected. Or it might be a traffic jam or

accident, or rain that ruined your parade or a sunny day that ruined your ice-skating trip. Whatever it is, think of this trigger that caused a disruption to your ordinary world. How did you respond?

There are many things in this life that we can't control—we can't control nature, the weather, or our biology, and we can't control the emotions, thoughts, words, and actions of others—but what we can control is how we respond to these things.

a. Do we choose to respond with fascination and build ourselves up?

b. Do we choose to respond with frustration and give up?

THE EXPERIENCE OF FRUSTRATION

A number of years ago my ordinary world was disrupted by a trigger outside of my control, and I didn't react very well to it. A counselor at the time explained that I was experiencing what was known as *situational* or *temporary* depression, yet my reaction to this situation over a period of nearly three years created what I would more appropriately call *persistent* depression. I was grieving not just the initial trigger but also the loss of who I once was, and this frustration eventually lead to the experience of hopeless despair.

Despite this, I still held onto an idea—an idea that I could choose to ignore or explore. Today I'm passionate about communicating this transformational idea with those who are experiencing frustration, confusion, discouragement, and despair, because it's an idea that has not only changed my life but has also sincerely saved my life. This simple yet transformational idea is Fascination.

I believe that choosing fascination over frustration is the key to enjoying the highest levels of happiness in life, and to understand how fascination works in this way we'll explore themes found in mythology.

THE HERO'S JOURNEY TO JOY

The Hero's Journey is a mythological concept that serves as a storytelling template to communicate the adventure, crisis, victory, and transformation of the main character or "hero." The concept was first introduced by the anthropologist Edward Burnett in 1871, later expounded upon by many others, and then popularized by the mythologist Joseph Campbell.[17]

We can see this pattern in storytelling, books, and movies, yet we can also view our own lives through this same mythological lens. By viewing life's circumstances as reflections of the Hero's Journey we naturally become engaged, active, and purposeful participants with life, rather than passive, disengaged, and uninspired spectators of life.

There are key words that serve as signposts for each phase of this journey, and these signposts form

---

[17] Campbell, J. (1949). *The Hero with a Thousand Faces.* New York, NY: Pantheon Books.

what are called *The 5 Levels of Happiness*, which can be understood as a happiness spectrum. For clarity, we'll unpack each of the five levels in context with the Hero's Journey:

The Ordinary World
The beginning of every myth is the experience of stability in the ordinary world—an ordinary world that heroes accept as their normal natural state. In the context of the happiness spectrum, the ground floor of both happiness and unhappiness are made up of the same thing, and that is acceptance. For our purposes we will define acceptance as the acknowledgment of what can and cannot be controlled. From this foundational vantage we can move up or down the happiness spectrum.

> The Ground Floor of Happiness is Acceptance.
> The Ground Floor of Unhappiness is Acceptance

Trigger
When a trigger disrupts the ordinary world heroes can choose to respond with frustration and give up, or respond with fascination and maintain curiosity to build themselves up. By choosing fascination heroes set into motion positive momentum.

> Level 1 of Happiness is Fascination.
> Level 1 of Unhappiness is Frustration.

Call to Adventure

Fascination with life's disruptions becomes a call to adventure! This is where curiosity leads to inspiration, with the creation of empowering dreams and goals as solutions to the disruption. Conversely, choosing frustration chokes curiosity, prevents inspiration, and leads to confusion.

> Level 2 of Happiness is Inspiration.
> Level 2 of Unhappiness is Confusion.

The Journey

Encouraged by empowered dreams and goals heroes become motivated to begin a journey towards the achievement of their supreme efforts! Conversely, confusion leads to discouragement, holding heroes back from taking motivated action.

> Level 3 of Happiness is Motivation.
> Level 3 of Unhappiness is Discouragement.

Ordeal & Reward

At some point during the journey heroes inevitably come face-to-face with their biggest challenges and receive their due reward. This success serves as positive affirmation to keep fighting the good fight! Conversely, discouragement can lead to the *negative* affirmation rewards of pity parties, victim-mentality-driven sympathy, and "misery loves company" attitudes.

Level 4 of Happiness is Positive Affirmation.
Level 4 of Unhappiness is Negative Affirmation.

Transformation

The final stage of the Hero's Journey is the transformation of the ordinary world to experience the highest level of happiness—Joy! This is where true enjoyment and excellence becomes possible due to the courage to take on the challenge of the transformational journey. Conversely, when heroes are content with the illusionary rewards of negative affirmation this can lead to the experience of hopeless despair.

Level 5 of Happiness is Joy.
Level 5 of Unhappiness is Despair.

FROM ACCEPTANCE TO JOY

After nearly three years of living in the dark night of the soul I embarked on a journey to crawl out of despair and back to the ground floor of acceptance. Once back on solid ground I resolved to make better choices moving forward, and the first choice was simple yet profound. Instead of being frustrated by the triggers that disrupt my world I chose instead to be fascinated by them. In so doing I became the hero of my own story, inspired and motivated to answer the call to adventure, presenting the opportunity to grow and become more than I ever dreamed I could be and experience the highest levels of happiness!

IF YOUR LIFE WERE A MYTH

Seeing your life as a myth is an exciting perspective. It's like living a fascinating book or movie! It's also fun to wonder who would play you in the movie version of your life. For me it would definitely be the versatile, prolific, and genius actor Eddie Murphy—because if anyone could pull it off it would be him.

If lately you've been frustrated, confused, or discouraged, then I encourage you to try Fascination on for size. As you do, you may find the following myth-related prompts helpful:

1. If your life were a myth, how would you describe your ordinary world?

2. What trigger is disrupting your world? Are you frustrated or fascinated?

3. What's your call to adventure? What are your dreams and goals?

4. Have you begun your journey? If so, what's motivating you? If not, what's getting in your way?

5. What rewards are you seeking? What positive affirmations have you already received? Are there any negative affirmations that might threaten to hold you back?

6. What kind of transformation are you working towards? What Joys have you already experienced?

It's been many years since I first worked through those prompts myself, and today I am stronger and happier than I've ever been. Even still, I can say with authority that disappointments still hurt, and sad things still cause tears; but, I can also say with confidence that what I learned in the process of digging myself out of despair has given me a perspective that makes the low points of life seem a little less low, and makes the dark days seem a little less dark. And that has proven to be a greater experience of magic than any sleight of hand or smoke and mirrors ever will be.

Final Thoughts

No one and no thing can make you enjoy life, and no one and no thing can make you excel in life. Enjoyment and excellence are personal choices that you choose when you're fascinated rather than frustrated, and when you take what you know and you take what you've been given and you do something amazing with it. As a lasting piece of encouragement, I leave you with the words of Joseph Campbell:

> "The cave you fear to enter holds
> the treasure you seek."

The Positivity Papers: Volume 1

3 QUESTIONS TO ASK YOURSELF BEFORE JUMPING INTO ACTION

— Issue 11 —

*T*here's a story attributed to Christopher Columbus that says when he sailed across the Atlantic to the "New World" there were those who criticized him, saying that anyone could have made the same voyage. To this, Columbus simply replied: "Yes, but I am the one who actually did!"

This story may or may not be true (as with many of the stories we've been told about Columbus) but its sentiment points to a common truth: whenever someone does something significant there will always be someone to rain on the parade.

During my formative years as a magician the urban shaman David Blaine became a household name with his 1997 television special *David Blaine: Street*

Magic.[18] The special did something unique by emphasizing the exaggerated audience reactions rather than focusing on the magic that Blaine performed. Before the show was even over I could already hear magicians the world over chastising the 24-year old magician, accusing him of having no stage presence and only using standard magic props. The overwhelming consensus was that any other magician could have been the star of the show.

We could debate the validity of their arguments, or acknowledge how the ego is always willing to work overtime, but this would ignore the fact that if something is possible then there will always be empowered people to bring it to life. Yes, many magicians could have made audiences scream, laugh, yell, and jump up and down on camera the way Blaine did, but in 1997 it happened to be David Blaine who actually did it.

MULTIPLE DISCOVERIES

In science there's an idea known as multiple discovery or simultaneous invention. This is when multiple people discover or create the same or very similar things simultaneously and independently. Popular examples include:

---

[18] Blaine, D. (1997, May 19). *David Blaine: Street Magic*. New York, NY: ABC.

- The formulation of calculus by Isaac Newton and Gottfried Wilhelm Leibniz.

- The discovery of oxygen by Carl Wilhelm Scheele, Joseph Priestley, and Antoine Lavoisier.

- The creation of the theory of evolution by Charles Darwin and Alfred Russel Wallace.

An incredible modern example of this is found in literature. The author Elizabeth Gilbert, in her book *Big Magic*, tells the story of a book she started to write but never finished. *Evelyn of the Amazon*, as it was tentatively titled, was to tell a harrowing tale:

> "It's about a spinster from Minnesota who's been quietly in love with her married boss for many years. He gets involved in a harebrained business scheme down in the Amazon jungle. A bunch of money and a person go missing. At which point her quiet life is completely turned into chaos. Also, it's a love story."[19]

Despite doing extensive research for the book, Gilbert never finished writing it. Not long afterwards she learned that one of her colleagues, Ann Patchett, had published her own new book, *State of Wonder*. Can you guess what this latest book was about? The book's summary was *identical* to Gilbert's unfinished book! Despite knowing nothing about Gilbert's book, Patchett had independently "discovered" the story herself! Instead of being angry or jealous about losing

---

[19] Gilbert, E. (2016). *Big Magic*. New York, NY: Riverhead Books. p. 53

her book to another author, Gilbert gracefully recognized the oft-quoted maxim: *"Ya snooze, ya lose!"*

From magicians lamenting over losing the chance to have their own television special, to an author's story finding another writer, the lesson is clear: if something is possible then there will always be empowered people to bring it to life. So if you have an idea, a dream, or a goal, and if you don't act on it, then surely someone else will!

The ego is always willing to work overtime, and if left unchecked our default reactions will lean towards jealousy, resentment, anger, or the like. It may even lead to an illusion of superiority, which essentially echoes the words of a famous song:

> "Anything you can do I can do better! I can do anything better than you!"[20]

WHY THIS MATTERS

Recognizing and accepting that we won't always be the first to do something—and that we won't always be the best at something—is imperative for maintaining mental and emotional well-being. What's more, sometimes what we think we want isn't really in our best interest. There are only so many hours in the day and so to be most effective in our lives part of our work is to focus on the activities that are best suited to our skills, interests, responsibilities, and motivation.

---

[20] Berlin, I. (1946). "Anything You Can Do."

3 QUESTIONS TO ASK YOURSELF

When faced with a myriad of amazing possibilities, we have the choice to ignore them or to explore them, and if today you feel called to start something new then I encourage you to ask yourself these 3 important questions:

1. Can I do it?
2. Should I do it?
3. Will I do it?

CAN I DO IT?

This is a confidence question. What it really means is:

> "Do I currently have the skills and talents necessary to do what it is I wish to do?"

This first question is a trick question, though, because if you've ever had the opportunity to see me speak at a conference or facilitate a workshop at a professional development event, then you know that I encourage my clients not to ask "Can I" because the question contains inherent doubt, with the power to hold you back even before you get started. Words have power, and so the better question is *"How Can I?"* This question is a build-up question because it presumes that there is a way and your task is to simply find what that way is.

If your answer to this question is "I can't" or "I don't know" then that doesn't mean it's the end of the story. It may mean you just have to find the answer or acquire the necessary skills.

SHOULD I DO IT?

This is a clarity question. What it really means is:

> "Is this an ethical and a valuable use of my time?"

Just because you are empowered to do something that doesn't mean that you should do it. Perhaps it would be unethical. Perhaps you just don't have the interest or passion for it. Or perhaps there are other things that demand your attention and so it's best to leave whatever it is you were considering to those who are more qualified with skill, interest, and time.

WILL I DO IT?

This is a courage question. What this really means is:

> "Do I want it bad enough, even it means overcoming my fears?"

When your desire for something more is stronger than your desire to maintain the status quo, you will become motivated to jump into action. Put another way, you are far more likely to step into your calling when the cost of *not* taking action outweighs any potential cost *of* taking action.

FINAL THOUGHTS

Whether you're a magician or an author, a CEO or a general manager, an entrepreneur or anything else, it's important to remember that if something is possible then there will always be empowered people to bring it to life. You may not be the first, you may not be the best—and it may not even be the best use of your skills, interests and time—but you'll never know until you stop ignoring it and start exploring it.

What's your latest idea? What amazing gift to the world are you sitting on? If you don't act on it today, then surely someone else will. Whatever it is that you are inspired to explore today, I encourage you to not ignore it. Instead, ask these 3 important questions to put your ideas, dreams, and goals to the test:

1. Do you have the necessary skills?
2. Is it a valuable use of your time?
3. Do you want it bad enough?

WHY POSITIVITY MATTERS
AND HOW TO EXPERIENCE MORE OF IT

— Issue 12 —

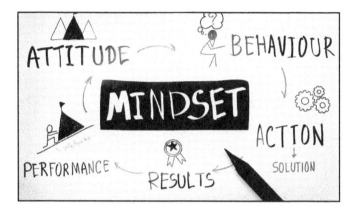

*W*e're living in a time hungry for people to think, be and stay positive. The world needs individuals from all walks of life to step up and lead with positivity for the benefit of themselves and for those within their sphere of influence.

Our lives are filled with conflicting influences, with some influences that can be considered "positive" and other influences that can be considered "negative," and still other influences that are neutral and are best understood as opportunities. From there we have a simple choice: to respond positively with fascination to create outcomes that are constructive, or to respond negatively with frustration to create outcomes that are destructive. The appropriate response can be made clear when we consider that many disciplines have suggested that negativity has a greater impact than positivity. For example:

- In finance it's said that losses have more of an impact than gains.[21]

- In psychology it's said that people tend to remember negative experiences more so than the more positive ones.[22]

- And in linguistics it's said that people tend to pay more attention to negative words rather than positive or neutral ones.[23]

The affects of negativity can be far reaching, and since these affects can be far worse than their corresponding positive influences, I suggest that this is a strong case for making positivity an intentional initiative rather than a happy happenstance, by focusing our choices to create outcomes that are constructive rather than destructive.

To paint a clear picture of the consequences of negativity in our lives, here's a brief outline of some of these effects on our work, on our relationships, and on our health:

---

[21] Kahneman, D. (1992). "Advances in Prospect Theory: Cumulative Representation of Uncertainty." Journal of Risk and Uncertainty, 5:297-323. Kluwer Academic Publishers.

[22] Tugend, Alina. (2012, March 23). "Praise Is Fleeting, but Brickbats We Recall." New York, NY: New York Times.

[23] Estes, Z., & Adelman, J. S. (2008). Automatic vigilance for negative words in lexical decision and naming: Comment on Larsen, Mercer, and Balota (2006). *Emotion, 8*(4), 441-444.

WORK

People spend a substantial part of their lives at work, and the quality of their workplace experience inevitably reflects in the quality of their lives. A single instance of a negative influence in the workplace can have a huge effect on an organization.

More than just a morale killer, according to a recent Gallup study[24] negativity in the workplace costs the economy between $450 and $550 billion dollars annually! Negativity in the workplace is a communal effort. If we don't step in to counteract it, then we are supporting it with our silence. Here's a brief summary of the consequences of negativity in the workplace:

Teamwork
When attitudes aren't in alignment stresses occur that lead to resentment and hostility, which can be expressed as gossip, lack of empathy, lack of understanding, or lack of communication.

Attitude
Negative workers can tend to have a "just a job" attitude where they only do "just enough" to keep their job rather offering energy and innovation to move an organization forward.

---

[24] Clifton, J. (2017). "State of the American Workplace." Gallup.com

Attendance

When the workplace isn't a positive place to be workers look for an escape, whether through genuine stress-induced illness, or through inappropriately used sick days. According to some estimates this costs upwards of 9% of payroll.[25]

Retention

When the workplace is a source of negativity team members will look for opportunities to jump ship, costing an organization lost productivity and revenue as new employees are recruited and trained. According to some estimates the average internal cost of turnover ranges from 30% to 40% of an entry-level employee's annual salary, 150% of a mid-level employee's annual salary, and up to 400% of a highly skilled employee's salary.[26]

When we choose to employ positivity principles and practices in our work, not only do we provide an environment and culture conducive to effective collaboration, but we also take responsibility for setting a good example for ourselves and for those around us.

Because negativity has such a far-reaching effect on not only our attitudes but also on the bottom-line,

---

[25] Wolfe, I. (2012, June 16). "How Much is Employee Absenteeism Costing Your Business?" SuccessPerformanceSolutions.com
[26] (2019). "A Step-by-Step Guide to Calculating The Exact Cost of Turnover." SparkBay.com

it follows that taking positive preventative action is a must.

RELATIONSHIPS

The environment and mindset that we have at work can impact our relationships outside of work, by influencing our behaviors and attitudes among our personal relationships, among both family and friends.

It's been said that people tend to rise or fall according to the sum total of their social circle, meaning if you spend a significant amount of time with a certain quality of social connections, whether they be positive, negative, or neutral, their influence will be seen in your own attitude, behavior, skills, and ambitions.

Just like in a workplace setting where one Negative Nancy or Negative Ned—or one Frustrated Francine or Frustrated Fred—can drag down an entire workplace culture, so too can just one negative individual in a social circle have a detrimental effect on the morale of the entire group.

Negativity among friends and family can present itself in subtle ways. It can appear as allowing destructive behavior to go unchecked, but it's disguised as wanting to be nice or not wanting to "rock the boat," or risk offending. It can come as complacency and stagnation, holding each other back out of fear of change. It can appear as playful jeering that when gone too far can lead to more overt negative consequences.

These more obvious impacts can lead to misunderstandings, resentment, being over critical of others all while ignoring our own shortcomings. It can lead to "coldshoulders," silent treatments, ghosting, gossip, and a severe lack of perspective, understanding, and empathy. Most of all it robs us of enjoying the precious time that we have with those most dear to us.

When we choose to employ positivity principles and practices in our relationships, we end up choosing carefully who we associate with, and we become a positive influence for those around us.

Because negativity has such a far-reaching effect not only on ourselves, but also for the people within our sphere of influence, it follows that taking positive preventative action is a must.

HEALTH

These negative influences have just as much damaging impacts on our health. Stress-induced illness[27] is a real thing that can lead to a weakened immune system, a decrease in pain tolerance, and an increased risk for heart disease. While those are the extreme consequences caused by negativity, some of the less

---

[27] Glaser, R.; Kiecolt-Glaser, J. K. (2005). "Stress-induced immune dysfunction: implications for health." *Nature Reviews Immunology*, Volume 5, p. 243–251

severe effects include anxiety and depression—which alone can lead to further negative consequences in all areas of life compounded by a poor attitude, decreased confidence, and lowered ambition.

Another conditioned caused by negativity that doesn't get talked about as much is something called stress cardiomyopathy—a condition with similar symptoms to a heart attack and which results in your heart not working as well as it should.

All of these health risks caused by negativity can further lead to increased stresses in your relationships and in your work, which only adds more fuel to the cycle of negative influences.

When we choose to employ positivity principles and practices to our health, we do all that we can to remove or reduce negative influences that can potentially hold ourselves back from achieving the level of enjoyment and excellence that we deserve.

The affects of negativity can be far reaching—on our work, on our relationships, and on our health—and since the affects can be far worse than their corresponding positive influences, it follows that we should seek to be more intentional about our choices to create outcomes that are constructive rather than destructive.

THE HASHTAG POSITIVITY DIFFERENCE

How would your work be different if your workplace culture was a positive place to be? How would your relationships be impacted if you and the people you connect with practiced positivity principles by design rather than defaulting to negativity? How would your health be transformed if you made more constructive choices? We may not be able to control everything that happens to us, but we are empowered to choose how we respond to our circumstances to facilitate positive outcomes.

According to one study[28] it's suggested that 50% of our happiness or unhappiness is outside of our control—a "set point" decided by our DNA. 10% is decided by our "circumstances"—the environments we find ourselves in and the things that happen to us. The remaining 40% is decided by our "intentional activity"—the choices that we make, whether by default or by design, in response to our DNA and our circumstances. Choosing positivity practices that are constructive rather than negativity practices that are destructive can truly be a game-changer for our life experiences.

While it is far easier to understand this intellectually, it is certainly much harder to practice when we're in the trenches of life. That's why it's important to remind ourselves every day of why we've chosen to be committed to building ourselves up rather than tearing ourselves down. Make a daily habit

---

[28] Lyumbirsky, S.; Sheldon, K. M.; Schkade, D. (2005). "Pursuing Happiness: The Architecture of Sustainable Change." *Review of General Psychology*, 9(2), 111–131

of giving yourself time to reflect on why positivity matters for you and the people in your life. Maybe it's a quote you frame on your wall, a knickknack you keep on your shelf, an image you us on you mobile phone screen, a card you keep on your wallet, or a note you keep on your bathroom mirror. Any reminder that you keep front of mind far outweighs the ones that you don't set for yourself.

THE FIVE TO ONE RATIO

Because negativity has such a bigger impact on our attitudes and behavior, it stands to reason that negating a negative experience will take more than a single positive experience. For example, researchers[29] studying relationships have found that a ratio of five to one is ideal in balancing negativity with positivity. In other words, for every one instance of criticism, contempt, defensiveness, refusal to cooperate or communicate, and the like, there must be five instances of interest, affection, appreciation, empathy, perspective, jokes and laughter, and the like. This study found that "as long as there was five times as much positive feeling and interaction between husband and wife as there was negative…the marriage was likely to be stable over time."[30]

---

[29] Benson, K. (2017, October 4). "The Magic Relationship Ratio, According to Science." Gottman.com
[30] Ibid.

How might you be able to use the five to one ration in your own relationships? How could you use it at the workplace? And how might it apply to your health?

Final Thoughts

Positivity matters because *we* matter. Each and every one of us is uniquely poised to make the world around us better simply because we are here. To help facilitate these positive experiences a good place to start is by making better choices that build us up at work, in our relationships, and for our health.

BONUS MATERIAL

— THE 5 C'S OF EXCELLENCE —

In the fall of 2018, I produced a five-episode series of *Magic Words*[31] outlining practical ideas for pursuing and achieving excellence in all areas of life. Excellence in this context is to be understood as not just *doing* our very best but actually *being* our very best. Achieving excellence, then, is marked by when our supreme passions and supreme efforts are met with supreme authentic character.

As a Magic Word, Excellence is a reminder that instead of just *going* through life, we should instead *grow* through life, calling us to not merely accept *wishful* thinking (desiring a better future but being unwilling to do anything about it), but instead embrace *hopeful*

---

[31] hashtagpositivity.com/magicwords

thinking (desiring a better future and taking calculated steps towards enacting positive change). By making this way of Being and Doing a lifetime habit we become enabled to compound truly excellent results.

The following selections are concise renditions of The 5 C's of Excellence as first published on the Magic Words platform. These five principles are Creativity, Clarity, Confidence, Courage, and Commitment. As you read through these you are encouraged to watch the companion videos online, which will contain additional resources.[32]

Enjoy!

---

[32] online.hashtagpositivity.com/excellence

The Positivity Papers: Volume 1

THE 5 C'S OF EXCELLENCE
— NUMBER ONE —
CREATIVITY

When I was a young boy my mother used to make costumes for me and my brother, and every year without fail we'd end up winning some sort of best-costume award. The idea of a store-bought costume simply didn't exist in our household, and looking back I think it probably had more to do with financial limitations rather than any sort of artistic integrity, yet this limitation is perhaps what most inspired my mother's creativity, enabling us to stand out from the crowd.

Whether you're making a costume, writing a book, starting a business, or collaborating on a project, tapping into your creative mind to see hidden possibilities despite real or imagined limitations can help you to make connections in places you never before could have considered.

The Magic Word Creativity reminds us that to pursue excellence means standing out from the crowd. As one of my mentors, John Maxwell, often says, we live in an age where we can win some races by standing still! Sometimes simply showing up to the arena is all you need to do to win because many people are simply not interested in putting in the effort to even show up! Going the extra mile truly sets us out from the crowd and, best of all, there's far less traffic on that extra mile.

REFLECTIONS

1) In what areas of your life do you stand out the most? What makes you so creative in these areas?

2) In what areas of your life are you the least creative? How are you blending in?

3) Make a list of all the ways you could be more creative to stand out from the crowd. What aren't others doing that could be your game changer move?

4) Choose one item from your list and commit to doing it. How did you stand out?

THE 5 C'S OF EXCELLENCE
— NUMBER TWO —
CLARITY

*I*n October 2018 I spent a week in Las Vegas where I worked closely with the leadership team of Wyndham Desert Blue, one of the city's newest resorts. What I most appreciate about this team is their dedication to excellence, and where they really excel is in the Magic Word Clarity.

Aside from the three hours we spent together in an intensive corporate Hashtag Positivity workshop,[33] I also spent two nights at the resort as a guest. During that time I challenged myself to guess what their Intention Statement is. An Intention Statement is a blunt statement that speaks to core values and desires. If you want to uncover your own Intention

---

[33] hashtagpositivity.com/workshops

Statement then a good place to start is by answering this simple questions: What effect do you want to have on others? In other words, how do you want others to be different because of you or your work?

Think of this as a one-sentence summary of your life's purpose. Or your company's purpose. Or the purpose of whatever activity it is you're working on. Truly, an Intention Statement can apply to anything and everything. You could write an intention statement for writing an email, for cooking dinner, driving to the store, or meeting with a friend, or truly anything else!

I've heard it said that Robin Williams had a poignant Intention Statement, evidenced in the phrase he'd often say to others: "Don't be afraid." Even his journals are said to be riddled with the blunt statement: "I want to help others to not be afraid." Now *that* is an intention statement! How beautiful that this gifted man was able to use his humor and kindness to encourage others in such a unique, memorable, and meaningful way. And that's the key for an intention statement—it gives you clarity to leverage your activities in a memorable and meaningful way that you are uniquely positioned to employ. What's your Intention Statement?

By the time I left Las Vegas I believe I figured out Wyndham Desert Blue's Intention Statement. They want to help welcome people home. With this kind of intention they don't consider their resort to be the typical Vegas hotel; rather, they see it as property owned by the people who stay there, and the workers are simply helping to keep the place running smoothly. Every time someone walks through the front door they are not simply walking into another hotel; rather, they are truly coming home!

Knowing their Intention Statement gives the Desert Blue team clarity to identify unique ways to bring that intention to life without being held back by the "default" activities that might otherwise keep them from making a real difference in the lives of the people they serve. In this way the Intention Statement can help identify the activities that can be eliminated in order to stay true to the desired effect without being marred by design.

The Magic Word Clarity reminds us that our days are filled with conflicting influences, so in our own quest for excellence, after we've used our creativity to explore all the amazing possibilities, our next step is to take some time to reflect on what our desired effect is, and then leverage our energy accordingly.

REFLECTION
1) Identify the area of your life that could use more clarity. Write an Intention Statement for this area.
2) List everything you can think of that can contribute to this intention. Remember to use your creativity!

3) List everything that's in your schedule for this coming week and reflect on whether your current time and energy is contributing to your Intention Statement.

- Are there activities you might want to add to your schedule?

- Are there activities you might want to take out of your schedule?

The point here is not to create overnight transformation, but rather only to serve as an opportunity to gain clarity on what is most important, and see where you might want to make changes moving forward to more effectively meet those self-prescribed values.

THE 5 C'S OF EXCELLENCE
— NUMBER THREE —
CONFIDENCE

A study[34] at the University of Wisconsin found that people with higher levels of confidence exhibit a greater willingness to take on risks and an enhanced ability to adapt to circumstances. This study seems a bit redundant, though, because by definition are not confident people those who are willing to take on risk and adapt to their circumstances? It's perhaps an obvious finding, yet it's also one that is worth exploring. For many people a lack of confidence is the primary cause for what's holding them back from growing into who they might be. And there are logical reasons for this, the chief of which is that it's all too

---

[34] Greno-Malsch, K. (1999). "Children's use of interpersonal negotiation strategies as a function of their level of self-worth." Milwaukee, WI: University of Wisconsin.

easy to lose confidence if we're not intentional about our growth and development.

In the book *Body Magic* by John Fisher[35] there's an activity that highlights just how easy it is to lose confidence, while also providing a suggestion for how to build it back up. This activity uses two sets of anagram cards, with three cards in each set. People are divided into two different groups. Group A gets one set of anagram cards, and Group B gets another set. The challenge is to see which group can solve their puzzles the fastest.

If I was working with you in a workshop setting I'd just have us all play the game together, but for the sake of explanation I'll just tell you the outcome: Group A wins every time. This outcome has nothing to do with Group B's ability; rather, it has everything to do with how the cards are stacked against them. Here's the setup: The first two words in Group A's set are TAB and LEMON—easy to solve anagrams. The first two words in Group B's set are WHIRL and SLAPSTICK—impossible anagrams. Group B could not solve their anagrams because there was nothing to solve! Having failed twice, this group gets stuck in a groove where failure becomes preconditioned, whether they're conscious of it or not.

Finally, when the third and final puzzle comes around, what the players don't realize is that both

---

[35] Fisher, J. (2014). *Body Magic*. Lanham, MD: M. Evans & Company.

words are the same. Both Groups A and B are given the same word: CINERAMA. Because Group B has been preconditioned to fail they presume failure is inevitable and don't exert much effort to solve the puzzle, while Group A is able to solve the puzzle with little effort because they had been preconditioned to succeed. Even though just seconds before this experiment began the people in Group B would have likely been able to solve the third puzzle with little to no difficulty at all, in only a matter of seconds their confidence was zapped preventing them from succeeding at even a simple task. That's how easy it is to lose confidence.

This same kind of conditioning is found in our everyday lives when we allow difficulties and disappointments to keep us from making progress, preventing innovations, hopes, and dreams from becoming a reality. Yet all we have to do is get out of the groove that expects failure and instead get into a groove that expects success by setting ourselves up with quick wins through reachable goals.

A simple strategy for building confidence is to ask the question "How Can I?" instead of asking the question "Can I?" The two questions sound similar but they have a clear difference: "Can I" contains inherent doubt, undermining our efforts before we even begin, while the question "*How* Can I" assumes that there is a way and we just have to find it.

When we invest in the development of our confidence we arm ourselves to be both willing and able to take on risks, and more able to adapt to changes. To help you in this development, consider the following:

REFLECTION

1) What area of life are you most confident? What makes you so confident in this area?

2) What area of life do you exhibit the least amount of confidence? What might you learn from your strengths to set a new groove for hopeful success?

3) What quick win can you achieve this week to make an immediate and valuable impact on your growth?

The Positivity Papers: Volume 1

THE 5 C'S OF EXCELLENCE
— NUMBER FOUR —
COURAGE

*I*n the short term it's always far easier to keep things the way that they are, even when making positive changes. Yet in the long-term it's always easier to actually make those changes, even if they're uncomfortable. These positive changes are what I like to call "gifts to our future selves."

For example, let's say you're thinking about procrastinating something important, but when you remind yourself that you're probably not going to want to do it later either, as a gift to your future self, you just decide to do it now. Or perhaps you consider skipping a workout, but when you remind yourself that your future self will want to be in good physical shape you decide to get up off the couch. Or perhaps a fear of the unknown and a desire for stability is causing you to reject an amazing new opportunity because everything worthwhile will always require risk. By reminding yourself that neglecting amazing opportunities will always cause your future self to wonder "What If," as a gift to your future self you decide to take calculated action steps despite any fears of failure or instability.

As T.S. Eliot points out, *"Only those who risk going too far can possibly find out how far one can go,"* and this Magic Word reminds us that the only way to build our strengths is to have the courage to take action.

Consistently. Boldly. In other words:

> "Whatever you can do or dream you can, begin it. Boldness has genius, power and magic in it. Begin it now."[36]

REFLECTION

1) Is there a difference between strength and courage? When are you in your strength zone? When are you in your courage zone? Is it possible to demonstrate courage in an area of your life where you are weak? Can you demonstrate strength even when you're not exhibiting courage?

2) What gift are you giving your future self today? Is it a gift you're looking forward to receiving?

3) What proverbial amazing opportunities are you currently missing out on because you allowed the

---

[36] Attributed to the writer and statesman Johann Wolfgang von Goethe

fear of uncertainty keep you from becoming who you most want to be? What changes will you make to give your future self a more valuable gift?

THE 5 C'S OF EXCELLENCE
— NUMBER FIVE —
COMMITMENT

*N*o matter your intentions, without Commitment any of the work you've done up until this point will not matter one bit. It will be as if you didn't do anything at all. This is tragic, because the road to excellence isn't easy. It takes guts. Sacrifice. Boldness. Our deepest fire of intention—the mark we want to leave on this world—will never come to be unless we keep moving forward by employing this Magic Word. In other words, when our conscious and unconscious minds are in disagreement, we literally hold ourselves back from commitment to anything in the long-term. When this happens, we give up without ever finishing what we started.

There can be many reasons for why we might give up too soon. Perhaps it's harder than we thought it was going to be, or is taking longer than we thought it would, or perhaps the circumstances changed and along with it our convictions also changed. Whatever the case may be, let's ignore the excuses for now and instead explore a strategy for staying motivated, inspired, and fascinated.

The more reasons you have for doing something, the more likely you will be to actually commit to it. Studies have shown that people tend to remember negative experiences over positive experiences, and that they will work harder to avoid pains over gaining pleasures.[37] This suggest that if you purposely reflect on your past failures to commit it can serve as an anchor for the associated negative emotions, acting as a built-in emotional hook to stay the course.

REFLECTION

1) Make an inventory of all the things you gave up on too soon. Next to each item, list all the things that might have been had you committed to following through.

2) For each item on you list, indicate how you feel about the outcome. Are there some things that you don't mind missing out on? What items do you wish you had worked out differently? What will

---

[37] Tugend, A. (2012, March 23). "Praise Is Fleeting, but Brickbats We Recall." PsychologyToday.com

you do moving forward when faced with similar situations?

3) Studies[38] have show that you are more likely to commit when you have passion for what you are doing. List of all the ways that your commitments relate to or support your talents and interests.

4) Lastly, outline all the benefits that are gained by following through in each area, including the rewards that others will experience as well. Research[39] has suggested that helping others is a valuable source of happiness, and so focusing on how your commitments will help all parties involved will armor your convictions for staying the course.

---

[38] Raab, D. (2017, June 12). "What's Your Passion?" PsychologyToday.com

[39] Lohmann, R. C. (2017, January 29). "Achieving Happiness by Helping Others." PsychologyToday.com.

The Positivity Papers: Volume 1

THE 5 C'S OF EXCELLENCE
TYING IT ALL TOGETHER

*"People often say that motivation doesn't last.
Well, neither does bathing—that's why
we recommend it daily."*

— ZIG ZIGLAR

When you engage in **creative** planning and develop greater **clarity** of purpose—and when you have **confidence** in your abilities, the **courage** to begin, and the **commitment** to follow through—you become poised to excel in all that you do!

••••••••••••••••••••••••••

While in pursuit of excellence have you or anyone you know ever experienced these kinds of triggers?

- Frustration with a difficult colleague, peer, or family member.

- Confusion over purpose or direction.

- Discouragement from critics or from past failures.

- Prolonged complacency or stagnation.

- Despaired the loss of a job or loved one.

No matter what triggers may be holding you back, Hashtag Positivity has a comprehensive approach to personal growth that is strategically designed to help you master the principles and practices necessary to transform your life by facilitating positive experiences at work, in your relationships, and for your health. This mindful process will coach you to consciously choose fascination over frustration in every situation so you can more effectively connect with others, gain clarity of purpose, manage change, and overcome adversity.

By investing in yourself with sincere effort you will gain two invaluable assets to carry in your proverbial toolbox that will transform your experience of the world around you. These two assets are Psychological Capital and Emotional Intelligence.

PSYCHOLOGICAL CAPITAL

Psychological Capital is a set of characteristics associated with better performance, stress reduction, and improved overall well-being.[40] These include:

Hope
Perseverance toward achieving goals the ability to and redirect one's path in order to succeed. When you have hope you are fully *engaged* in all that you do.

Efficacy
Possessing the confidence to take on challenging tasks and put in the necessary effort to succeed by adapting to ever-changing circumstances. When you have efficacy you are fully *empowered* to take consistent action.

---

[40] positivepsychologyprogram.com/psycap

Resilience

The ability to sustain and bounce back from adversity to attain success. When you have resilience you are *encouraged* to stay in the game to celebrate success.

Optimism

The ability to have a positive outlook about succeeding in the moment and in the future. When you have optimism you *enjoy* all aspects of your life.

(NOTE: When you employ all of these characteristics you become your own H.E.R.O. Now that's something worth striving for!)

EMOTIONAL INTELLIGENCE

Emotional Intelligence is the ability to "identify, understand, use, and regulate emotions in life,"[41] and is comprised of the following competencies:

---

[41] Jones, M. (1997, September 1). "The Unconventional Wisdom of Emotional Intelligence." PsychologyToday.com

Social Skills

Influence through clear and persuasive communication tactics, relationship building, change management, and valuable shared experiences. When you have honed social skills you are *engaging*.

Self-Awareness

The ability to recognize your own emotions and their effects and acknowledge your self-worth and capabilities. When you have self-awareness you are *empowered* to succeed.

Empathy

The dedication to service of others by assisting in their growth and development, along with a commitment to discerning the emotions behind their needs and wants. When you have empathy you are able to provide *encouragement* to others.

Discipline

The ability to manage negative disruptive impulses, maintain honesty and integrity, take responsibility, and be adaptable. When you have discipline you *enjoy* life free from distractions.

Motivation

The commitment to personal growth and development with optimistic initiative and resilience. When you have motivation you are committed to *excellence*.

MINDFUL GROWTH

If lately you or your team has been feeling frustrated, confused, discouraged, complacent, or despondent—and if you're ready to move to the next level—then give a gift to your future self by scheduling your complimentary Positivity Breakthrough Session today to gain the character, competencies, and capabilities necessary to fuel transformation! Get started today at:

HashtagPositivity.com

FINAL THOUGHTS

This volume has explored how positivity can impact our everyday lives by addressing a myriad of issues: From ways to become more engaged, empowered, and encouraged; to the importance of choosing our legacy now; to suggestions for improving our relationships; and more. The information found here is not meant to be a final say on these topics, but rather as a living and breathing conversation. You are encouraged to contemplate how you see your own life circumstances reflected in these issues and, more importantly, you are encouraged to actually apply them to your life. This can perhaps seem overwhelming at first glance, but the important thing to remember is to simply start with where you are, start with one thing, and start making positive changes.

As you begin to reflect on this process here's a simple suggestion that may prove helpful:

First, take out a piece of paper and a pen and write down a list of the twelve issues from this volume.

Second, rate yourself on a scale of 1 to 5 of where you are today in each of these areas. Write this number next to each topic on the list. For clarity, you would rate yourself as a "1" if you are consistently terrible with the topic in question, and you would rate yourself as a "5" if you are consistently perfect in that topic.

(NOTE: If you rate yourself as a 5 in any of the topics then you may as well give up in that area because you will never be able to improve any further. However, if you rate yourself as a 1 in any of the topics then this is a very encouraging revelation because you will never be able to get any worse!)

Third, reflect on your findings. Where do you excel the most? What needs the most improvement? Why do you think that is? Where might you want to begin making changes?

Focus

As you consider your findings, also consider something my mentor John Maxwell teaches in his book *Leadership Gold*:

> "I've known people who thought that reaching their potential would come from shoring up their weaknesses. But do you know what happens when you spend all your time working on your weaknesses and never developing your strengths? If you work really hard, you might claw your way all the way up to mediocrity! But you'll never get beyond it."[42]

Mr. Maxwell reminds us that our life purpose will never be found in our weaknesses because we are never called to do something for which we have no talent. Therefore, consider that your call to action after doing this exercise might not be to focus all of your

---

[42] Maxwell, J. C. (2008). *Leadership Gold: Lessons I've Learned from a Lifetime of Leading*. Nashville, TN: Thomas Nelson. p. 59

attention on the areas that you marked as a 1 or a 2. Perhaps, instead, a better and more fruitful use of your time will be found in focusing on what you marked a little higher. Perhaps.

This does not insinuate that we should completely ignore our weakness, only that perhaps we will find more enjoyment and rewards by focusing a little higher. For example, I'm a horrible chess player, but that doesn't keep me from having a chessboard on my coffee table, ready to play when visitors come by. While I have no aspirations to be a Chess Grandmaster, I do hope to play a game or two every now and again. In other words: "Make your strengths effective and your weakness irrelevant."[43]

Additional Resources

Zig Ziglar is quoted as saying: "People often say that motivation doesn't last. Well, neither does bathing—that's why we recommend it daily." I believe this is true, and so to encourage you to stay motivated I've made a number of additional resources available for you. Enjoy!

WORKSHOPS

Workshops facilitated by Hashtag Positivity provide in-depth knowledge, skills, and resources to emerging leaders and their influencers to develop resilience in the face of life's challenges. Topics include fostering a

---

[43] Attributed to the management consultant and author Peter Drucker

growth mindset, gaining clarity of purpose, and developing high value relationships. Learn more at:

hashtagpositivity.com/workshops

ONLINE COURSES

Online courses offered through Hashtag Positivity provide invaluable access to positivity tools and strategies anywhere that internet is available. Login using any computer or with your mobile device using our mobile app. See what positivity can do for you, all at your own pace. Give it a try today at:

learn.hashtagpositivity.com

VIRTUAL GROUP COACHING

Group coaching through Hashtag Positivity provides access to a world-class curriculum along with the collective knowledge and experience of the group members. Sessions are facilitated virtually through weekly group conference calls and check-in emails, along with a dedicated social media page for ongoing networking. Give it a try today at:

hashtagpositivity.com/coaching

PODCAST

The world is full of negative news stories, that's why the *On a Positive Note* podcast looks to what's right with the world first and then uses that knowledge to make what's wrong with the world better a little bit better (or maybe even irrelevant). Tune in and subscribe at:

hashtagpositivity.com/podcast

VLOG
Every week Hashtag Positivity releases a new coaching video outlining a single positivity principle to employ in everyday life, weeding through distractions, giving you concise ideas to facilitate positive experiences. Give it a try today at:

hashtagpositivity.com/vlog

BLOG
Every month Hashtag Positivity curates the latest positivity research, publishing the findings in accurate, accessible, and actionable practices for thinking, being, and staying positive. Read the latest articles at:

hashtagpositivity.com/blog

BOOKS
Every year Hashtag Positivity publishes at least one new title to the community to spread positivity principles and practices that are accurate, accessible, and actionable Browse the collection today at:

hashtagpositivity.com/books

Moving Forward
Remember, because you read this book I am now on your team and you are now on mine. Just as the Grand Canyon would never have been created had it not been for its relationship with the Colorado River, so too will our own Grand successes not be possible without leveraging the unique gifts that each and every one of

us has to contribute to the greater good. If you have any questions or comments, or any relevant stories to share, email me at jonas@hashtagpositivity.com to continue the conversation.

The ball is in your court! Let's play!

Enjoy —

"Reading is a conversation. All books talk. But a good book listens as well."

— **Mark Haddon**

ADDITIONAL TITLES

The Positivity Papers: Volume 2
(2020)

The Positivity Papers: Volume 2 is the continuation of Jonas Cain's ongoing research into the science of positivity. As a the second book in the series, this work continues the tradition of curating principles and practices for making the world a little bit brighter in a way that's accurate, accessible, and actionable. Along the way the author shares a few of his own adventures (and misadventures) in applying these strategies, which readers will find both informative and at times entertaining.

The Positivity Papers: Volume 1
(2019)

Positive thinking is often viewed as the practice of wearing so-called "rose-colored glasses," pretending that everything is fine and dandy even when everything isn't fine and dandy. But can choosing to overlook reality really be considered "positive thinking?" Can the experience of a good lie really be a *good* thing? And can what we don't know—via genuine ignorance or willful blindness—actually hurt us?

The Positivity Papers: Volume 1 is Jonas Cain's work to confront these issues by curating research on the effects of positivity and negativity on our work, relationships, and health. Along the way he discusses practical principles and practices to employ this research into our everyday lives and shares his own personal experiences in applying these stratagems, which readers will find both informative and at times entertaining.

Magic Words
(2018)

Within the pages of this book you'll find a collection of principles for conjuring personal and professional growth that's taken Jonas over two decades to compile. Each word is fully explained to help readers quickly and easily implement these ideas into their daily lives. Read it straight through cover-to-cover, or keep it on your nightstand for daily encouragement—either way *Magic Words* is an excellent source for empowerment and encouragement to Boldly Step Forward Perform!

Are You P.O.S.I.T.I.V.E.? Rethinking Positive Thinking
(2018)

Positivity is often misunderstood to mean putting on a pair of rose-colored glasses, pretending that everything is fine and dandy, even when everything isn't fine and dandy. But Jonas Cain holds that this understanding of positivity is flawed, arguing that true positivity can not ignore reality but instead has to reflect an honest assessment of the truth.

Are Your P.O.S.I.T.I.V.E.? will take you on an 8-step journey that will encourage you to "rethink positive thinking," opening you to a life of engagement and empowerment!

...and the Pursuit of Happiness
(2017)

What does it mean to be happy? Is it a physical sensation of pleasure, or if it more of an attitude? Is it resiliency won by virtuous living, or is it satisfaction with the state of affairs? Can we be happy even if don't feel happy?

This book examines these questions by exploring various theories of happiness from philosophical and practical perspectives, while also exploring the author's own earnest attempts at applying these theories. *...and the Pursuit of Happiness* is a concise guide meant to help you rediscover Happiness again for the first time. Are YOU ready to be happy?

Absurd Jokes
(2016)

Inspired by the time Jonas figured out the meaning of the term Pittsburgh Steelers, after being mugged on the streets of Pittsburgh, this book suggests a mathematical equation for humor: TRAGEDY + TIME = HUMOR

This edited compilation of Jonas Cain's all-time favorite jokes aims to offer readers inspiration to find solace in the humor of life's tragedies.

The Problem of Poverty
(2016)

By examining the individual and structural causes of poverty, and the political, religious, and ethical perspectives of society's obligation to the poor, this preliminary study aims to suggest an innovative course of action to deal with this social problem. This proposed prescription will have a focused emphasis on individual responsibility implemented in pockets of localized communities that when duplicated across regions will demonstrate significant national success.

Just Another Day
(2015)

The long awaited sequel to *It Just Happened the Other Day: A True Story*, this book opens on just another day for Jonas Cain as he embarks on a cross-country bicycle ride, from MA to L.A. Detailing his ensuing detours, this book highlights that the actual destination truly matters little when you're on an adventure.

Journey of Discovery: Awaken Your Inner Power
(2010)

A book you can read in an hour or keep on your nightstand for daily inspiration, *Journey of Discovery: Awaken Your Inner Power* offers concise practical ideas for bringing your inner purpose to Light. If approached with an open heart and an honest mind, this material is sure to help you on your journey to awaken your inner power.

It Just Happened the Other Day: A True Story
(2010)

One day two best friends decided to write a book together. Before a word was even written they already had a title for it. Whenever Stephanie told a story she would begin by saying, "It just happened the other day," even if it had actually happened months earlier; and whenever Jonas told a story he would begin by saying, "It's a true story," even when what he was saying was actually a joke. Due to unforeseen circumstances, the pair never got to write their book...until now.

A poignant true story of love, loss, and inspired hope, *It Just Happened the Other Day: A True Story* is sure to touch the heart of all readers.

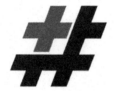

RESULTS

"I was not expecting it! My roommate and I have exams coming up this week and we were both really anxious going into it and after watching the show we kind of took a deep breath and we got more positivity out of it. The magic tricks got me, they for sure got me! But I really liked the reality aspect of it and that we got positivity out of it, and just it was great!"

Kailyn Helgeson, Student
University of Minnesota Duluth / Duluth, MN

"He was amazing! The group loved him and his message. His delivery is such a creative and fun way to get such strong and important messages through. The world needs more Jonas Cain's in it! He's the type of person you want to be around all the time. Positivity runs in his blood! We are managers of assisted living and memory care communities. We need positivity and laughter to be able to provide the highest quality of care to our residents. Jonas made us laugh, think and be in the moment."

Angela Pelletier, Director of Operations
WoodBine Senior Living / Marriottsville, MD

"Jonas gave an hour-long keynote to the Sigma Alpha chapter of Phi Mu Alpha Sinfonia at UMASS Amherst. He met with myself and two other members of our executive committee and discussed what our organization stands for as well as what we hoped to get out of his presentation, and then created a presentation customized to what we discussed. To say that the chapter was pleased is a tremendous understatement. His presentation had the whole group laughing and learning about ourselves and one another. When we adjourned that evening, the group was better connected and more cooperative than it was when we opened. I recommend Jonas Cain without hesitation or reservation for any workshops, keynotes, and coaching sessions you may require. He is a tremendous asset to any team building exercise and you will be better having worked with him."

Robert McDermott, Educational Officer
Phi Mu Alpha / Amherst, MA

"Jonas Cain came to the Summer Summit for Driver Educators in Vermont and gave a customized motivational presentation that was just what I asked for giving time for driver educators to rethink what we do, get a fresh outlook on teaching, and start the school year running. Jonas accomplished this through the use of magic, engaging the driver educators early in his presentation. Having Jonas inspire a fresh outlook and an open perspective was a segue for the rest of our conference. The evaluations told me it was one of the best conferences we have had. The driver educators were charged up and received a lot of information, and activities, to take back to use in their programs in order to kick off the new school year. He left everyone a believer in how we can all improve as educators and people."

Nancy Andrus, Driver Training Coordinator
Department of Motor Vehicles / Montpelier, VT

"I've sat through many keynotes. It's very rare that a performer manages to capture my attention in a way that I can't help but be a part of the performance and be a part of the audience, and this performance did that for me! I was caught along by some of the magic tricks, I was caught along by some of the jokes, and it really connects you to the message in a way that I don't really get to see a lot, and getting to see that is really something that makes this conference amazing!"

Jacob Jones, Alumnus
Texas TSA / Fort Worth, TX

"The students truly enjoyed Jonas Cain's presentation. He was funny and entertaining. Most importantly, he communicated an amazing and positive message using his magic tricks in which all the students could relate to and make their own!"

Sister Kathleen Marie, Principal
St. Denis-St. Columba School / Hopewell Junction, NY

"As a client of Jonas Cain's, I can say that he is a great coach, teacher, and magician! After just two sessions of Jonas' positivity training, I was mind blown on how much positivity can change how you look at everyday problems and how you can solve them. I used to get very upset over little things and wanted to just give up after things got hard but with this training I have learned to stay positive in every situation and stop looking at all the negatives of the situations or the 'what if 's,' but to look at the situation and the positives of it, and how a positive mindset makes a huge difference. I highly recommend his positivity training to others because it can help anyone and everyone."

Heather Scott, PCA
Tempus Unlimited, Inc. / Ware, MA

"Through some mix of his demeanor, gentle but targeted prodding and compelling course material, Jonas opens up a class of young people to speak with confidence and without fear of judgment, despite having just met one another. I cannot overstate how impressive this is. I've continually found Jonas Cain's work to be consistently compelling."

KC Fussell, Legislative Aide
Massachusetts State House / Boston, MA

"What makes Jonas Cain's presentations stand out from the rest is that he doesn't just deliver an empowering message; instead, he also actively engages his audience with interactive magic, inspirational stories, quick wit, and charm, making for a truly memorable and meaningful experience for our community. We always look forward to the days when he is with us! I highly recommend Jonas Cain if you're looking for an engaging, empowering and highly encouraging experience for your group."

Orly Munzing, Founder & Executive Director
Strolling of the Heifers / Brattleboro, VT

"Jonas was the kick start to out Kindness Day at our elementary school. His charisma and welcoming demeanor grabbed the students' attention right away and kept it for the entire performance! Jonas' message of kindness and positivity was sprinkled throughout, effortlessly. The connections he made with magic and having good character are lessons that will last a lifetime. Both adults and students were amazed by Jonas' talent. Most importantly, Jonas loves what he does and that shines through from beginning to end!"

Molly Cole, School Psychologist
Hatfield Elementary School / Hatfield, MA

"Nearly moved me to tears! It was an emotional rollercoaster that left me with a different perspective on life and how to live it. Before the show, I had nearly given up on many of the life goals. After that night however I was shown that you can achieve just about anything if you stick to it. Jonas is a man I will not soon forget. He and his story is one I shared with just about everyone I know."

Corbin Armstrong, Student
UMASS Amherst / Amherst, MA

"I found so much value in this presentation. Not only was it engaging, but all of us got something out of your training. As a director, I found information specifically helpful in working with my staff. However, even my youngest and newest staff got useful information and tips. The training was so beneficial for every level of employee we have and already am finding the information useful."

Heidi Gutekenst, Director
Belchertown Day School / Belchertown, MA

CONNECT WITH JONAS!

f / jonascain

◎

▶ / jonascain

🐦
in / jonascain

Foster a positive mindset, gain clarity of purpose, improve your relationships, and develop resilience!

Receive weekly positivity resources and take the exclusive Positive Self-Assessment. Best of all, it's free to give it a try!

HashtagPositivity.com

ABOUT THE AUTHOR

Jonas Cain is the owner and Chief Facilitator of Fascination of Hashtag Positivity, LLC. His passion is supporting emerging leaders and their influencers to develop resilience through a positive mindset, clarity of purpose, and improved relationships.

He studied magic at the McBride Magic & Mystery School, social ethics at Salem State University, and Learning Design & Technology at Purdue University, and is a certified coach, trainer, and DISC Consultant with the John Maxwell Team.

The author lives in Massachusetts and in his spare time enjoys traveling, climbing mountains, and spending time with his cat, Pumpkin.